Spring Creek Chronicles

Stories of Commercial Fishin', huntin', workin'
and people along the North Florida Gulf Coast

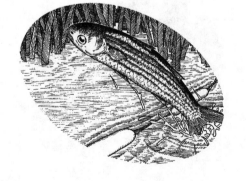

Spring Creek Chronicles

Stories of Commercial Fishin', huntin', workin'
and people along the North Florida Gulf Coast

Written by Leo Lovel

Illustrated by Clay Lovel

Edited by Ben Lovel

Leo V. Lovel
Tallahassee, Florida

Library of Congress Catalog Card Number: 2001 126434

ISBN 0-9709616-1-8

Leo V. Lovel
Spring Creek Restaurant
33 Ben Willis Road
Crawfordville, Florida 32327
(850) 926-3751

ACKNOWLEDGEMENTS

First and foremost, I must acknowledge the Lovel family, from my grandparents all through the line to my nieces and nephews, including all my in-laws. A hardworking, caring and stick-together bunch as there ever was.

Second, I must thank and acknowledge Mother Nature who has so generously provided us all with so much.

Third, I wish to recognize the proud, independent, commercial fishing families of the North Florida Gulf Coast that have been strong enough, brave enough and smart enough to make a living from the sea.

Last and very, very least, I must acknowledge the Florida Marine Fisheries Commission and the Florida Marine Patrol. With their ridiculous rules and constant harassment by land, sea and air they finally managed to take our commercial fishing licenses for ninety days, after a two year court battle. This inspired us and gave us the time to write and illustrate these stories.

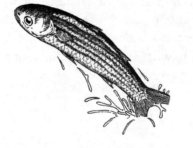

INTRODUCTION

Spring Creek Chronicles is a collection of sixty or so short stories, observations and opinions gathered from a life of living and working on the North Florida Gulf Coast.

The community of Spring Creek is a small commercial fishing village located at the end of County Road 365 that deadends into the Gulf of Mexico. Two fish houses, one church, forty or fifty residents and Spring Creek Restaurant make up the town. Commercial fishing, crabbing and oystering have been the backbone of the economy forever. The freshwater springs here pump 1294 million gallons of water a day and dump it directly into the gulf. Saltwater fish, freshwater fish, oysters, shrimp, crabs, alligators, otters, ducks, birds of every kind abound in the bay. Deer, turkey, bear, hogs and all the woods animals there are, live along the shoreline.

These stories give an insight into the habits of most of these creatures and some of the people of the area too. I'll never be able to put into words the excitement, the fear, the beauty, the wonder and the craziness of it all.

Enjoy these stories, cause we sure enjoyed livin' em.

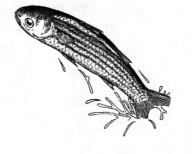

Contents

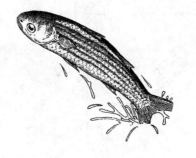

MY OLD MULLET SKIFF   CLAY MARSHALL LOVEL   7-   -99

My Old Mullet Skiff

My old mullet skiff is probably old, as mullet skiffs go. Bruce and I had it built the year Nathan was born and he'll be nineteen soon.

Wish I could see, in one big pile, the fish it's carried home, wish I had 10 cents for every hour I'd spent in it.

Wayne Householder built that boat for us in 1980 out of marine plywood and cypress. We've replaced the front bulkhead (where the motor is) twice, the stern once, and patched numerous holes and splits. All this due to the constant rough use of the boat in commercial fishing.

The boat itself is nineteen feet long, about six feet wide across the top, with the motor, a 40 horse Yamaha, stuck down in a tunnel or well in the front of the boat about four feet from the tip of the bow. This set up allows for you to be able to strike and take up a net from a large six-foot by six-foot deck on the stern of the boat.

We almost always toted about six hundred yards of monofilament, some times as much as eight hundred yards if we were carrying our trout net with us too.

The ice box, fiberglass, that would hold five to six hundred pounds, sat in front of the net table, the fuel tank in front the ice box, the motor ahead of the fuel tank, and me, ahead of the motor, standing on the bow, twisting the handle wide open on that 40, cruising the bars and channels looking for a buncha fish.

That boat took it.

For nineteen years that boat's been slammed on oyster bars, grounded on the beach and swamped, sunk in big rains, beat, bounced and abused yet it still brought home loads of fish – mostly a few hundred pounds of fish, sometimes only dozens of pounds of fish, sometimes thousands of pounds of fish.

It always brought something home.

Deer, alligators, eels, crabs but mostly fish, mullet, trout, redfish, pompano, mackerel, butterfish, shark.

That boat carried my wife, two children, playpens, highchairs, groceries, nets and me, back and forth to Dog Island, four miles offshore of Carrabelle.

That boat's had a cullin table laid across the rails and been loaded with tongued oysters when times were tough.

Two teenage boys learned the bay, Ben and Clay, in that ole tunnel skiff, actually growing up on the back of that boat from the age of five or six.

That boat's been frozen, with ice on the deck, and burned up in one hundred plus degree temperature, so hot that the wooden floor crackles from expansion in the heat.

It rows good, with nine-foot ash oars, floats in four inches of water, runs in one foot of water and will carry two thousand pounds of fish, plus gear.

The original stern boards hang on the wall in my room, worn down paper thin on top from so many lead lines and corks being drug across it.

The boat's semi-retired now. Still functional as a commercial gill net boat, but now serving my boys as a bass and bream fishing boat with a little four horse sitting on the stern.

The boat seems happy and healthy when I get in it. The bottom's dry, the wood still strong. Looks funny though with cane poles, fly rods and cricket boxes in it, instead of nets and ice boxes.

That four horse on the back of the boat instead of that 40 on the front really seems odd.

The boat looks ready though, ready to trip a pile of net on the back, stick that motor in the well and go chase mullet.

Ready to go at the drop of a hat.

That's what it was designed and made for and that's what it wants to do.

Nineteen's old, for a mullet skiff.

I think the time of mullet skiffs has passed.

FEBUARY FOGGY DAY   CLAY MARSHALL LOVEL   6-8-99

February Foggy Day

February in North Florida is our worst month. Cold, dreary, wet and fog, lots of fog, especially on the coast. The water is warm compared to the air. The air is full of moisture and when conditions are right we get fog so thick you can move it with your hand.

Makes it tough to get around on the water.

Makes it just right, for a fisherman like me, to sneak out on low water, follow the oyster bars like a well-marked path and strike mullet in the holes with good old-fashioned monofilament net that the state out-lawed in ninety-five.

Loved that fog. It protected me like a warm gray blanket. Felt safe in it, secure in my lonesomeness, protected by its veil from prying eyes and the Florida Marine Patrol, who couldn't find me even if they knew I was out there.

I was doing my thing out by Carter bar.

I'd struck some fish, was clearing 'em out of the net, taking my time and enjoying myself, lost to the world in the gloom.

I heard voices.

Faint, but voices nonetheless, soft talking voices. Couldn't make out the words.

Surprised me a little, knowing nobody was out that I knew of.

Didn't worry me too much though, there was a bar between me and the voices and the fog was thick as soup.

I shucked the last fish, straightened my net up and decided I'd go check out some fish I'd seen in Old Creek the day before. I knew nobody could follow me and get there in this mess, I'd have trouble making it myself. If the fish were where I thought they'd be I could strike 'em and not worry about getting caught.

I jumped through the gap at Carter bar. There's barely enough water to run the boat in, the tide being so low. I wind that old forty horse wide open to keep from going aground. I guess the angle to run from Carter bar to hit the outside bars off Old Creek and I guess just right, cause I hit in about the Cedar trees on the Old Creek channel. I know right where I am now, even though I can't see fifty feet. I find the end of the oyster bar I'm looking for, run down it two hundred yards, see the fish whirl off the bar and strike my net.

All three hundred yards of it.

I wind the circle down good, to make 'em hit. Cut the motor off, walk back to the net table, grab the end of the net, stand up and notice the fogs lifted up about ten feet off the water.

I notice something else too.

I notice a little white boat with two black dressed men about five hundred yards away, looking at me with binoculars.

I start getting that net on the boat.

I mean I'm snatching it in like a man possessed. I'm shucking fish like a juggler keeping his balls in the air, leaving oyster-burrs, seaweed, logs and rocks in the net.

I look out at the Florida Marine Patrol.

They're running their boat as hard as they can across the shallow flats towards the Old Creek Channel. It's the only way into where I'm at. They can't come straight at me.

I'm getting' it on now, putting that net on the boat.

Mud, grass, seaweed, fish flying everywhere as I try to get cleared up.

I'm hassling like a racehorse that's run a hundred miles. I guarantee you could hear me sucking in air and blowing it out, like a train, at half a mile away with the effort I'm putting in.

My forearms start tightening and cramping, a prelude to my fingers locking up like claws. It's happened before during times of extreme effort.

I look up again and know I'm in trouble.

The FMP's run aground two hundred yards from the channel and they're out in the water pushing and dragging that boat as hard as they can to get to me.

Dedicated S.O.B.'s aren't they.

Fifty yards of net to go, twenty-five, ten, I snatch the staff on board and race forward to the motor.

My first reaction is to put the motor down and haul ass, but I realize there's no place to go. If I run up Old Creek on this low tide, I'll just run out of water and they'll have me boxed in.

I've got one chance.

One chance and one avenue of escape, but I've got to wait where I am just a little longer. I've got to watch the law drag their boat another fifty-sixty yards. Far enough so that if I do break out of Old Creek they'll have to drag back, the way they just came, and that'll give me enough time to make it to the dock.

Cause they can sure run me down.

My old forty won't run with their seventy-five on their little boat.

There's one little channel of water on the East Side of Old Creek. One little drain that holds eight to ten inches of water. It's got rocks and oysters in it, but if I can get the boat up and wide open before I hit it, miss all the rocks, I might get out on this side.

Now is the time, the FMP's better than halfway across the mud flat, dragging and pushing their boat.

Here we go.

Sideways slide around the end of the bar into that little drain.

6

Twisting the handle off the throttle to get more power.

Mud, and shell flying up through the tunnel. Pool ole forty horse a grinding and a screaming and trying to jump off the boat from the stuff I'm plowing it through.

Damn what a tough motor, twenty more yards and I'm outta here!

The prop bites good water.

We sound like a giant bee as I head for the dock as hard as I can go, only now looking back at the FMP.

They're standing there with their hands on their hips watching me go. Knowing they ain't gonna drag that boat of theirs back to deep water in time to catch me.

The old, deep, primordial yell comes from within me, an ancient sound, an animal sound, a sound that just comes out unbidden at certain times of victory like when you've stuck a good bunch of fish and they're beating the side of the boat off, trying to escape the net.

I race to the dock. Throw my fish on ice in the cooler, tear off my slicker suit and boots and disappear into my room to collapse, exhausted on my bed.

I'm wiped out from the physical exertion and the mental strain. Guess that's why all my hair's turned gray since ninety-five, why I've got gallstones and frayed nerves.

I fall asleep and sleep til time to take a shower and go to work at the restaurant. I come out of my room and my oldest son Ben approaches and says, "What's going on Pop, we got visitors out front waiting for us to open. They've tried the front door twice."

I look around the corner to see two Florida Marine Patrol trucks in the parking lot.

The waitress turns the closed sign to open and the FMP marches in, four of em.

I think I'll wait a few minutes, before I go to work tonight, see what happens.

Thirty, forty minutes pass and none of the help or the FMP comes hunting me.

I go in, get a cup of coffee and amble over by the table the FMP sits at.

Two of 'em look up, half smile and nod a greeting. They're the old-timers that don't mess with us too much if we don't throw it in their faces.

The other two law-dogs are new guys and they don't look too happy with me, sorta pissed in fact.

All four of 'em eating dinner.

The two old timers eating fresh fried mullet, hot from the grease.

The other two are eating crow.

Enjoy your dinner boys.

THE PELICANS LEARN A LESSON   CLAY MARHALL LOVEL   6-7-99

The Pelican's Learn a Lesson

I witnessed an encounter between two birds today that I found quite interesting.

This morning when I went down to the fish house to check on the boats and the ice machines, my blue heron buddy was waiting on me to feed 'em, as he usually is when we're around.

Since I was going in the cooler anyway, I picked up two small mullet heads, just the kind he likes, to throw to 'em. I stepped out the cooler door and threw one mullet head over the fish-cleaning table to where the old heron stood.

Before the old heron could take the two steps he needed to pick up the fish head, a pelican, that was perched on top of a piling in the canal, sails down from the piling onto the ground and stole that mullet head right out from under the herons beak.

I'd seen the pelican do this before.

Usually the heron squawks in protest.

Usually the pelican hisses in reply and swallows the fish head.

Usually.

This time the heron takes one step toward the pelican, silent as can be, and while the pelican is trying to swallow the fish head, the heron, with his six-inch long, inch and a half wide, hard yellow beak, lays one mighty peck to that pelican's head.

The pelican rises up straight, drops the mullet head from his mouth, and deflates like an old beach ball into a pile of brown feathers.

Dead as a stone.

With blood trickling out of a hole in the side of his head like he'd been shot with a .22 rifle.

The heron was shocked.

He stepped closer to the pile of brown feathers and looked it over close, twisting his head from side to side in obvious amazement.

I guess when he was satisfied that the pelican was no further threat, he picked up the mullet head that had fallen from the pelican's mouth and swallowed it.

I threw 'em the other head, and he leisurely picked it up and swallowed it too.

The coons had the pelican for supper that night.

SO MANY FISH   CLAY MARSHALL LOVEL   6-10-99

So Many Fish

Have you ever struck a good bunch of fish?

I mean get 'em just right, packed up tight in a ball from the cold, and in water the right depth where your net will stand up. A place where you can get 300 yards of monofilament all the way around 'em and have 300 more yards to wind 'em down with, in the circle.

It fires me up every time, no matter how many times I've done it.

Mullet so thick that a dozen jump over the staff when it hits the water.

Mullet so thick that they're beating the sides of the boat like a drum when you're winding 'em down. The cork line's turning to foam from the fish hitting the net and there's a roar that you can hear over that 40 horse Yamaha's whine of thousands of fish, in the air, in a flurry like snow as they pile over the corks. Fish so thick that you can't help but chop up a few dozen with the propeller on your motor as you put the net overboard.

Fish so thick that they jump in the boat.

Fish so thick that they hit you in the back, the head, you have to dodge 'em to keep 'em out of your face.

So many fish, that some primordial instinct takes over and a sound, a whoop, a yell comes from somewhere deep inside; a sound you can't duplicate under controlled and civilized circumstance, a sensation of being wild and free and what it must have been like to challenge mother nature all day, every day, with you and your family's and your villages well-being in the balance.

So many fish that you can't help but wonder about who put this master plan together and provided us with so much.

So many fish that you thank the Great Maker for being so generous.

So many fish.

I've struck that many fish, many times.

SNAKES, LAKE JACKSON   CLAY MARSHALL LOVEL   6-16-94

Snakes, Lake Jackson

Snakes; don't like 'em.

Scared of 'em. Been around 'em all my life in Florida. Just got where I don't kill every one I see like I used to.

I used to kill a lot of snakes.

Almost more than I'd believe if I hadn't been there.

I grew up north of Tallahassee, Florida on Lake Jackson. It was a great place back then in 1963 or 64. Bream, bass, duck hunting, frog gigging, trot line running, snipe shooting, anything you wanted to do on the water we had it.

One late February it started to rain and it didn't stop for about two weeks.

The lake rose and rose and rose, flooding people's houses, yards and barns, rising to where nobody could remember seeing it that high.

I guess the snakes hadn't counted on it rising that high either cause it flooded all their winter dens and made 'em take any high ground or bush they could find. Grape arbors, flower gardens, tree limbs, front porch railings, azalea bushes, anything that was out of the water, caught some sunlight and had a fork in it, snakes gathered on.

The snakes got in great bunches, all intertwined in big balls with 6, 10, 15, 25 snakes in a wad, all wrapped around each other trying to stay warm. I'd never seen 'em act that way before or since, and I don't want to.

These snakes drove our lakeside neighbors crazy and they wanted them dead or run off and that's where I came in.

I was 12 or 13 years old, loved to fish and hunt, loved to shoot as all boys do, had a bolt action .410 and just needed something to shoot at and shells to shoot with.

My good neighbors provided me with both.

Unlimited shells. They'd leave 'em in their mailbox for me to get after school.

Unlimited snakes. They'd leave them for me too in their flower gardens and fruit trees.

I remember coming home, getting my ole 410, my hunting vest, filling all my pockets with paper hulled, 3 in., number 7 _ shot shells, and hitting the neighborhood with 2 shells in the magazine and one in the barrel.

I'd shoot every snake I saw.

Single snakes swimming through the water, snakes curled up on floating grass and huge balls of snakes wrapped around each other in forks of trees.

I'd just fire in amongst those snakes in balls. One shot into the mass of snakes and as fast as I could jack another shell into that old .410. I'd shoot 'em, swimming away in every direction, reload and shoot til I couldn't see anymore or until too many of 'em would swim toward me in their panic and I couldn't shoot 'em all. I'd have to run away and blast at 'em from a distance.

I tried to keep count for awhile but after a couple of weeks and 250 to 300 kills I couldn't keep track, so I gave up trying to keep count and just hunted 'em unmercifully.

One day in particular I'll never forget.

The snakes almost got their revenge.

This event I'm about to relate did slow me down in my quest for more snakes to shoot, cause it scared the hell out of me. And I had a lot in me at that time.

What happened was one windy afternoon I'd taken a new tactic on snake killing. I was borrowing my neighbor's big wooden skiff and was letting the wind blow me through lily pads and weeds shooting snakes wherever I saw 'em.

Safer this way I thought, no wading through the grass or stomping through the bushes where one could sneak up and bite me.

Effortless too, just drift with the wind and shoot, shoot, shoot.

As I drifted through the weeds I noticed I was drifting up on a large area of windblown lake grass all piled up thick, too thick for the boat to go through and I stopped up against it.

"Look at that old dead mudfish", I thought as I spied a big brown lump, big around as a football with scales the size of my thumbnail on it.

"Look at that snake's tail laying up on top of that dead grass", as I spied something about six feet behind the dead mudfish.

"Look there's another dead mudfish poking up outta the grass two or three feet in front of the first one".

And look up there ahead of that, covered with weeds and grass was something that kinda sorta looked like a big, big, big snake's head.

But it couldn't be.

Not that big, bout the size of a round point shovel blade, couldn't be a snake.

Hell I got plenty of bullets, I'm not buying 'em anyway, I'll just shoot that round point shovel and see what happens.

Bam!

Something happened all right.

That round-point shovel was a snake's head. Those two dead mudfish about 10 inches in diameter were the body of the snake and that snake's tail behind 'em was a snake's tail alright, it was attached to that giant snake's head about 10 to 12 feet away.

Grass flew everywhere when that snake started writhing around after I shot 'em.

Bam, I shot 'em again.

Here he comes straight for the boat twisting and twirling and splashing and hissing, probably blind from the shots but coming fast.

Fast, you talk about fast, that 410-bolt action became an automatic.

Bang, jack another shell, bang, jack another shell.

Reload, reload.

He's coming up the side of the boat!

I'm standing on the seat on the other side of the boat.

Bang, bam, 3 feet away, in the head, 6 shots in this monster and he's done.

I'm about done too, I'm shaking so hard and in such a state of disbelief that I'm almost stunned.

Then I realize that I've got to take 'em home or no one will believe me.

I can't do it.

I can't touch that snake with my hands.

I can't grab that huge monster that's so terrified me with my left hand and hold that 410 with my right.

I leave and go home.

Mama's in the yard talking to a neighbor and I try to calmly tell her about it, but the point doesn't come across, trying not to act like I'm scared to death (not the manly thing to do).

So I've got to bring 'em home.

I get a yard rake.

I go back to the scene.

He's still there, still twitching a little bit as snakes do (till sundown so I'm told).

I hold the rake in my left hand.

I hold that 410, safety off, fully loaded in my right hand pointed at that dead snake.

Nervous, shaking again at the sight of this monster.

I try to hook 'em on the rake but he's so big he just slides off everyway I try to grab 'em.

Shotgun poised and ready at all times. I poke at him some more.

No good, he's sinking under the grass with every attempt.

Finally he's gone, sunk, like he's never been there.

I'm almost glad, a dream I've finally woken up from, it's over.

Four or five days later I come back and find that's he's floating up, as I knew he would do after a few days, as everything does when it starts to decompose, but the turtles and other scavengers had been after 'em and had chewed 'em in two.

I finally got the nerve to grab a piece of his tail and lift up a five foot section, which wasn't very impressive and smelled like the devil himself, and let it go.

I guess the proof will have to rest with me and my memory.

MULLET   CLAY MARSHALL LOVEL   8-9-99

Mullet

Poor ole mullet. Everybody and everything in the sea, air and on land loves 'em.

Did you know that they're one of the two vegetarian fish in the ocean, the sturgeon being the other?

By far the porpoise's favorite food. I've seen porpoise throw themselves out on the hill just trying to catch mullet that were hiding in the grass on the shoreline. Can't bait a crab trap with mullet. The porpoises will roll every trap over just to snatch the mullet out of the bait-well.

Pelican's dive on 'em when the mullet are trying to run down the river.

Eagles and osprey snatch every one that gets too close to the surface.

All your fish in the ocean eat mullet. From the trout feeding on the finger mullet in the estuaries to the marlin eating three-pound mullet off-shore.

Cormorants chase 'em underwater.

Seagulls pick up the small fry in the grass.

Gators eat 'em.

We strike 'em with our little bitty nets off the airboat.

Castnetters throw at 'em when they swim under the bridges.

I've seen pictures in National Geographic where the ancient Hawaiian Kings constructed huge stone holding pens in the bays around their castles to fatten their own private stocks of mullet.

We fry 'em, smoke 'em, broil 'em, bar-b-que 'em, grind 'em up and make dip out of 'em. We use 'em for crab bait, trout and redfish with 'em, troll for sailfish with 'em, even feed our pet blue heron when we have plenty.

I'd rather catch 'em than do any other outdoor activity that I know of.

I don't know why, but to put a net around a good bunch of mullet and watch 'em stomp the corkline down, fish jumping everywhere, gets me as excited today as the first time I struck some over twenty years ago.

We need mullet. Lots of mullet. Mullet of every size for the reasons I've mentioned above.

My customers, especially the locals and the older South Georgia bunch, have to have their fix of mullet, grits and hushpuppies at lease once a week or they get real nasty.

I know.

I'm the one they raise hell at when we're out at the restaurant, as we now seem to be most of the time as the crunch from the net ban and the ridiculous rules from the Florida Marine Fisheries Commission make it almost impossible for us to catch any.

Maybe it's not "poor ole mullet" anymore. They've got more protection now than us humans do from thieves and drug dealers.

They are the basis for the food chain in the sea, but they're also the basis for our food chain in this part of the coastal world.

We're having a hard time making it without 'em.

We see 'em out there, jumping on the rock piles, flipping along the grass. We see 'em hunkered down in the deep holes in the creeks in the winter. We watch 'em moving in great schools down the rivers and along the oyster bars.

They better enjoy their vacation cause we haven't given up on figuring a way out to catch 'em.

We love 'em too much, we want to take 'em home with us, we need to take some home with us.

It's a matter of pride and a matter of taste.

Good tastes or tastes good.

Whichever.

Boar Hogs Can Kill Dogs

We got into dog hunting for a short while. Somewhere along 1970 or 1972.

The only kind I'm familiar with is running deer, with walker hounds on St. Joe land or in the National Forest.

Bobby and I did this for a couple of years but the boring times, hunting dogs instead of deer, outweighed the exciting times and we went back to still hunting.

This is one of the exciting times that has stuck in my memory.

The Bufords, in Liberty County, had invited our whole dog hunting group to come and run deer on their property.

I got directions from Leon, my partner in the paint business and the person who'd gotten me introduced to dog hunting.

We all met up in one of the most sparsely populated counties in Florida, at a deer camp in the pinewoods.

One of the Bufords met us there, cooking homemade sausage and eggs, fed us up, made us feel at home and read us the rules.

"Enjoy yourself, kill every big buck you can, but don't shoot any of our hogs." "They're ranging free, wild and mean as hell, but try to leave 'em alone."

No problem, we're looking for a big buck, not much interested in hog no how.

We all split up to track the roads, staying in touch on the C.B.'s.

There's a big buck track, going from West to East. Leon and Red dump all the hounds out they've got on it.

There's three or four puppies, eight to ten months old. Some sorry dogs, that just follow but have good mouths when the deer's jumped. Then there's the real deer dogs. The backbone of the group. The ones with the nose and the voice. The ones that only bark when they smell something hot and they're on the trail.

Sweetning was the dog. When she barked her high-pitched yelp, there was something to it.

Ringo was a big male walker hound, with a deep brassy voice that only kicked in when he had seen the deer. He hung with Sweetning.

They dumped the dogs out. Sweetning and Ringo included. They trailed off into the pines and all hell broke loose.

Every dog opened at once. Must have been ten of 'em in there, barking, squealing, yowling like excited dogs do when they jump the deer.

All of us in trucks took off to the other side of the block of pines to cut the deer off. Me and Bobby set up on a long straight stretch of sandy road, jumped out and listened to the hounds giving chase at the top of their lungs.

What an experience that is! Standing there facing the woods with a whole pack of fired up hounds racing towards you. A chorus of barking, yipping, baying dogs getting louder by the second. Driving that ole deer along in front of 'em. The sound they make reaching back down the gene pool to some ancient, wild emotion that makes the hair stand up on your neck and your heart race. When you start hearing the bushes popping and breaking you really get focused then, cause that's the sound the deer makes charging through the underbrush, busting the bushes we call it.

This particular race (that's what they call it when the dogs are chasing the deer), the sounds of the hounds start swinging North, away from us, and eventually turns all the way around heading back west in the directions they came from, the deer making a big circle.

All the other hunters, in their trucks, load up and take back off for the other side of the block to try to get ahead of the deer.

Bobby and I, for some reason, decide to stay where we are, in case they double back again.

The sounds of the race are quickly fading away as the dogs push toward the west and we figure this race is about over for us.

Bobby yells and points up the road as a big, black boar hog, at full speed crosses the road and starts running down an old log road through the clear cut. Right behind 'em are Sweetning and Ringo, split off from the rest of the pack, and they're not saying a thing (barking), just running that big hog.

I fire up my old Chevy truck and we take off down the same road the hog and the dogs went down, soon catching up with the three of 'em.

Never before have we been able to observe the actions of the pursued and the pursuers from such a bird's-eye viewpoint. Usually all this is happening in the thick woods, but for some reason this old boar has taken to the road. The dogs have taken after 'em instead of the deer the rest of the dogs are chasing. Me and Bobby are right behind the dogs and the hog, watching this battle being played out.

The hog's running flat out. He's well over two hundred pounds and got an impressive set of tushes, or tusks sticking out of his lower and upper jaws. He's fast, but Ringo and Sweetning, walker hounds that they are, are much faster. They catch up to the boar and nip his flanks with their teeth like they're trying to hamstring 'em.

That's when the old boar shows his impressive fighting tactics.

Running at full speed, dogs nipping at his butt, the old hog locks his front legs and keeps running wide open with his back legs. Now, old Ringo and Sweetning or both, fixing to bite the boar in the butt, are running wide open into the hog's face and those fearsome tushes. With a grunt and a slash of his great head, the old hog throws one dog and then the other, ten feet through the air, cutting 'em with his tushes. He wheels around and takes off again, staying in the road. The dogs are up and after 'em again before you can blink an eye.

Fifty yards down the road the dogs catch up to the hog again and nip 'em. The hog repeats his previous tactic and cuts and throws both dogs again. They yip and howl from the bite of those tusks, and you can see blood running down their sides, but they never pause or slow down their pursuit. Soon as they can gain their feet from being thrown, they're hot after 'em again.

It was amazing to watch. The hogs timing and agility was incredible. Being able to turn around 180 degrees at full speed he used the dog's superior speed against 'em. When they realized they were facing that powerful head and tusks, they couldn't stop or even veer away before they hit. The hog always had his head held low and when his face was full of dog, he'd just lift it in a sideways motion, hooking those tusks in a belly or shoulder and seeming with no effort, cut 'em deep and throw 'em high.

The dogs were gonna die if we couldn't catch 'em off that hog.

They were addicted to the chase, bleeding, whimpering, limping but still giving chase. Old instincts taking over that wouldn't let 'em quit til either the hog died or they did.

Four or five times we watched the dogs take punishment. Each time trying to catch the dogs before they recovered from being thrown, but they were too fast.

The hog starts to tire and runs off the road and backs up to a deep furrow bank, facing the dogs. The dogs hesitate going in on that formidable, well armed head, and Bobby sails out of the truck and catches Ringo by the collar.

The hog grunts twice and charges Bobby. Bobby turns Ringo loose and dives into the back of the truck and the hog and dogs fight like hell, snarling, growling, grunting and squealing all three wrapped together in a tight ball, biting, slashing, cutting. The hog throws one dog, runs slam over the other one and takes off again.

The dogs are a little slower now, but still pursuing. Ringo's got some intestine poking out his side and Sweetning's got blood all over her but they just won't quit. You can't tell the hog's hurt at all, but he's tiring and has backed up again by a big stump. Ringo's facing him off and Bobby's finally got ahold of Sweetning.

I sail out of the driver's seat, ought-six rifle in hand. Jumping over the brush headed toward Ringo and the hog who are cussing each other in animal talk thirty yards from the truck. I'm yelling at Ringo to "come here" and believe it or not he backs up from that boar, thinking he don't want no more of that mean black hog.

I get ahold of Ringo's collar, watching that pissed off, bloody black hog all the time, knowing how fast he is and what he can do with that mighty head and shoulders, and those tusks. Ringo seems willing to be drug away and I'm thankful for that.

Then the hog diverts all his attention to me.

A loud grunt signals his charge as he bolts from the stump towards me.

I let go of Ringo and snap my rifle to my shoulder, finger on the trigger, looking down the sight.

Ringo backs up too.

The hog stops, twenty feet away.

"Go away hog," I say out loud, "I don't want to kill you." I'm a little nervous and scared after seeing Ringo's guts hanging out and Sweetning's shoulder cut where the white bone's showing thru. "Go on now."

We're both frozen in place. Me in the classic standing rifle position, leaning slightly forward, cheek pressed to the stock, tense, ready.

The hogs slightly crouched, hind quarters low, front quarters spread, head down to cut and slash. He's making little short grunts with every breath.

I admire that hog, his fighting ability, his speed, his toughness and tenacity and I want him to go away, to live. He deserves it, and Mr. Buford probably owns 'em, if anybody can "own" something so wild and fierce.

With a deep, loud grunt he charges.

I fire and he piles up going end over end from his momentum, to lie still in a cloud of dust, ten feet away.

"Get Sweetning loaded up," I yell as I drag Ringo back to the truck with me, sick at heart for more than one reason. I had to kill that noble animal and I'm going to have to leave 'em to keep from getting the whole Buford clan pissed off, and Leon and them losing their hunting rights.

I still feel bad about shooting 'em twenty years later, and I quit dog hunting not long after that. After another crazy experience, but that's another story.

That was a noble, tough, smart, dangerous animal that old boar was. I hope he fathered many little pigs that have the same spirit.

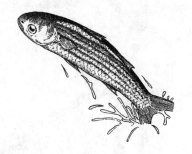

MR. CC   CLAY MARSHALL LOVEL   7-   -99

24

Mr. C.C.

Mr. C.C. is a retired commercial fisherman. He raised a family of seven children with a paddle skiff and some nylon pocket net. Catching mostly mullet, some trout during the winter, and anything else he could row that net around to feed his family.

He's about eighty-five now. He and Tootsie, his wife, had been married sixty-two years when she died a couple of years ago. He had stopped fishing when I first met 'em and had started hanging net for other fishermen. Everyday of the week you could see Mr. C.C. out stringing up cork line, laying out the lead line, unbundling the five and ten pound hanks of monofilament and tying in the webbing of the gill nets. Some were two hundred yards long, others a thousand yards long. A tedious, monotonous but skillful task.

I had hired C.C. a few times to hang nets in for me, when I first came to Spring Creek. I'd go up to check on the progress of the nets, always anxious for 'em to be done, and sometimes I'd help C.C. hang my nets. Him guiding me on how many meshes to put to the tie, how much drop to leave in the tie line, so on and so forth. I got to where I liked hanging net and have been hanging my own now for about fifteen years, but what I like as much as the net hanging was listening to C.C. talk about the old days when he was a young man in Spring Creek.

Mr. C.C. says there wasn't much to do around Spring Creek in Wakulla County, when he was young. No phones, no T.V., dirt roads and bad dirt roads, too bad to try and go anywhere on, and nobody had cars anyway.

Fish, hunt, raise a family and Mr. C.C.'s favorite, wrestle, was about all there was to do. Mr. C.C. says that young, strong men from all around the area would walk great distances to test out somebody they heard was a good wrestler. Each community had their favorite cause their favorite had whipped everybody else's ass and declared himself their favorite.

To listen to Mr. C.C., I think it was most likely that way with him too. Many times he told me about running his fishing partners up trees when he got mad or they played a joke on 'em. Them not wanting to let Mr. C.C. get his hands on 'em. They had felt his strength before.

I can just imagine what C.C. must have been like when he was young. Rowing that paddle skiff all over the bay, all his life, had developed arm, leg and shoulder muscles that still showed up in his old body. The grip he's got, when he shakes hands, will still make you shake back good and firm. Square shouldered and tall, missing one eye Mr. C.C. was, and is, maybe a little stooped now, but tough.

He told me they wrestled standing up, shirts off. They'd face each

25

other and on the word go, they'd grab each other, each trying for position, and try to "throw" the other to the ground, and that would constitute a win. Usually, the best of two out of three "throws" would end the match. C.C. told me that wrestlers came from quite a distance to try to "throw" him. St. Marks, Panacea, Tallahassee, Perry, Aucilla. Young men would either walk or hitch a ride to try C.C. out and go away dirty and dejected.

One day he was home at Spring Creek, close to the fish house he worked out of, when a man from South Georgia knocked on his door and asks for C.C. C.C. told 'em that he was talking to 'em and asked the Georgia man what he wanted.

The Georgia man said that he heard that C.C. was the best wrestler in the area and that he considered himself to be a good wrestler too, and wanted a match with C.C., there in the front yard, if he would be so kind.

Now C.C. said that he could look at the man and tell that he could whip 'em with no problem at all, and he really didn't feel like wrestling right then.

This upset the Georgia man a little but he remained calm and polite and explained to Mr. C.C. that he'd come a long way to wrestle and would really appreciate it if Mr. C.C. would give him a try.

C.C. refused again.

The Georgia man pleaded some more.

C.C. came up with an idea.

C.C. told the Georgia man that he would wrestle 'em on one condition. That condition was, that he had to wrestle C.C.'s oldest daughter first. If he could throw Jula Mae one time, then C.C. would consider the man fit to wrestle.

C.C. calls Jula Mae out of the house. Now Jula's no petite young woman. She's no fat young woman either. She's a teenage girl, broad across the shoulders, barrel-chested, strong arms and legs.

The Georgia man's flabbergasted.

He ain't never wrestled no woman before, much less a girl, and he ain't going to do it.

C.C. tells 'em that's the condition and if he wants to wrestle 'em, he's got to throw Jula first.

Jula's ready, shirt on of course, legs braced one behind the other and wide apart for balance, arms spread towards to the front, fingers extended.

The Georgia man consents. He wants C.C. bad and if he's got to throw this girl one time, he'll do it. He tells C.C. that he'll try not to hurt her.

C.C. tells him, he better try not to get hurt. That Jula's damn good herself.

The Georgia man squares up with Jula, looking kinda apprehensive and takes his fighting stance.

C.C. asks 'em if they're ready. They both nod and C.C. says "Go".

They clinch, Jula throws the Georgia man over her left hip in the blink of an eye.

The Georgia man lands in a cloud of dust, flat on his back, immediately jumping up and saying that he'd held back cause it was a girl and he wanted another try.

Jula's grinning and proud, ready to go again.

C.C. says he can try it again, since he's come such a long way.

Georgia man's squaring up with Jula again. He's embarrassed, he's mad, he's confused and he's ready. Veins popping out, red faced. A girl's done thrown his ass flying and now he's gonna show her.

C.C. asks, "Ready?"

They both nod again and he says, "Go".

They clinch, struggle, groan and strain for about two heartbeats and Jula throws the Georgia man again, except this time over right hip.

Georgia man lands on his back again, jumps up and yells "You bitch" and slaps Jula Mae. C.C. jumps off the porch where he's standing, grabs Georgia man by the shoulder, spins 'em around and cold cocks 'em with a big right fist to the mouth, laying 'em out, unconscious this time, in the dust again.

C.C. gets Jula Mae, tells her what a good job she did wrestling and they go back in the house.

C.C. told me again that he could tell by looking at 'em, that Georgia man wasn't worth his time.

We're both hanging net, counting meshes, tying knots, counting meshes again. C.C.'s talking about old matches he'd had. This one he'd fought, that one he'd fought, where they'd come from, where he'd went. Bragging about how good he was, how strong he was back then. How he'd never been beat, never.

Then I noticed he was thinking about something.

Then he looked over the net at me with his one good eye and told me that there was one time. One time he'd had to say "uncle" or give up, but it wasn't really a fair fight and it really wasn't wrestling.

I told C.C. that he'd have to explain that one to me.

This is what he told me.

Erwin was C.C.'s younger brother. They paddleboat fished together when they were not much more than boys.

C.C. said that he and Erwin had been fishing all night around the oyster bars at the mouth of Spring Creek. It was almost daylight and C.C. was pushing or rowing the skiff home. A frost was on the marsh grass, the creek steaming from the cold weather. They hadn't caught hardly anything and Erwin was curled up shivering in the bow of the boat.

27

A mullet gets up and flips by the marsh grass up in front of the boat. Another fish jumps and then another one.

C.C. stops rowing and tells Erwin to get up and take the staff to the hill.

In the old days of paddleboat fishing, you had to take the end of the net or the "staff" to the shoreline to pen up the fish. This was done by one man jumping in the water and wading to the bank dragging the end of the net with 'em. This was what C.C. was telling Erwin to do on that freezing cold, pre-daylight morning.

Erwin says, "No, it's too cold".

C.C. tells Erwin again to get the staff to the hill, there's a big bunch of fish right in front of the boat.

Erwin says he ain't going and curls up tighter.

I told you before that I think C.C. pretty much ruled the roost around there as far as men his age went because of his size and strength. Most times he could intimidate Erwin and the others to do his bidding and this was one of those times.

"Erwin, you get that staff and you take it to the hill or I'm gonna come up there and stomp your ass and throw you out".

"I ain't going, C.C.".

C.C. said he threw down the oars, took the two steps forward to where Erwin lay, grabbed wide-eyed, scared Erwin by his coat collar with his left hand, and drew back his right fist to whollop 'em.

Erwin, afraid of the beating he's fixing to get from his brother that's standing over 'em, reaches up with both hands and grabs C.C. by the balls, squeezing tight.

C.C.'s instantly frozen in position. Fist cocked back, hand full of collar, legs spread wide with Erwin holding on for dear life.

"Let go", C.C. says, sounding mad and surprised.

"I can't C.C., you'll kill me if I do".

"Let go Erwin", C.C. says, getting madder but is helpless.

"Won't do it", Erwin says, tightening up a little in his fear.

It's a standoff C.C. told me. Neither one moving at all. The boats drifting in the current, the sun starting to rise, the fish still jumping in front of the boat.

"You've got to let me go", C.C. barely manages to get out in a whisper, he's in so much pain, and if he moves at all Erwin tightens up more.

"Say uncle and swear you won't beat me if I let you go".

"Uncle", whispers C.C.

"Say it again, louder", Erwin says.

"Uncle", C.C. tries to shout.

"Swear you won't hurt me", Erwin says.

28

"I swear I won't hurt you", C.C. manages to croak out.

Erwin turns loose, C.C. gets his breath back and they rowed home.

"That's the only fight I ever lost", C.C. tells me.

"Did you beat Erwin's ass?" I ask.

"No, I'm a man of my word", C.C. replied, picking up speed on his net hanging. "Probably beat his ass later for something else, but not for that".

Mr. C.C. can't hang net anymore. I think his eyesight probably stopped that. He sits rocking on his porch, not able to see me when I drive by and wave. I have to honk now when I pass by, to let 'em know that he was there.

My First Hunt Alone

My dad, Ben Lovel, started me out hunting and fishing. I remember going with him from the time I was so small that I couldn't do much more than watch. Daddy loved to duck hunt and I tagged along anytime he'd let me, cried when he wouldn't.

I remember when I got old enough to carry a B.B. gun on the wood duck hunts. Then daddy bought me a bolt action .410 and under his close supervision I got to shoot at the Bluebills that flew down the lake by where we lived.

What a thrill, to be shooting a real shotgun at flying ducks, I must be growing up now.

My next real goal was to be able to go hunting by myself and this is what I remember about that first trip.

I grew up on Lake Jackson north of Tallahassee, Florida, in Leon County. No better place could there be for a young boy that loved the outdoors.

Many mornings I'd wake up to the sounds of ducks, wings whistling, some quacking, geese honking. I'd lay there in bed in the pre-dawn grayness and dream of the time that I could just jump up, grab my gear and gun, and go to the lake. I could picture in my mind's eye what it looked like standing in the dog fennel on the edge of the lake. Hundreds, maybe thousands of birds would be flying. Some high up, in V's traveling. Many more would be buzzing up and down the lake in groups of two to two hundred, going in every direction of the compass, mingling in the air to make clouds of birds. Some separating, some lighting on the lake, others going on somewhere else.

We never had decoys, we didn't even have a blind. Didn't need 'em. Just go down to the shore, find some bushes to hide in, and fire away. Every once in awhile you'd hit one.

One cloudy winter afternoon, I was playing in the yard and the duck were burning up the air, so many were flying in and out of the lake.

I went inside to try to talk Daddy into taking me down to the lake so we could shoot a few.

To my great surprise he told me to go ahead and get ready, bring my gun to 'em so he could go over all the safety features with me, and that he didn't feel like going, but that I could go by myself, if I promised to be careful.

I couldn't believe it. Boy was I excited.

I'm finally becoming a man at the ripe age of twelve.

I got my shell vest. Counted the seven, number six shot, three inch

.410 shells twice, to make sure I had 'em all. We bought our shotgun shells for a nickel each back then. I can remember buying 'em two or three at the time from Red and Sam's bait and tackle on North Monroe Street. Got my old hand-me-down camo hat, my rubber boots, my trusty .410 and I was ready.

Daddy went over all the things I needed to do to be "safe", and said for me to go on if I wanted, but don't load up til I got to the lake.

What an adventure. I'd walked through our yard and down to the lake a thousand times to hunt and fish, but never had I walked alone with a gun.

I felt different. Taller maybe. Older maybe, definitely more mature and grown up.

Things looked different or maybe I was just paying more attention cause I had to look out for myself, make my own direction instead of just following Pop and obeying his commands.

I crossed the dirt road in front of our house, slipped through the Geheres' side yard and before me was duck-filled Meginnis Arm, a big long slough on the south side of Lake Jackson.

I could see a bunch of coots feeding in the lily pads along the shoreline and there was my first prey, a small pod of Bluebills diving and feeding in the grass in the shallow.

Time to load up.

I'm cool as a cucumber as I put one shell in the barrel and stuff two more in the magazine of that mighty .410.

I'm kneeling in the bushes loading up and now I'm tuned in on those birds in the water.

Creep along slow, bent over as far as I can, to keep from being seen. I've got no problem with shooting 'em on the water if they'll let me get close enough.

Peek my head up over the bush tops.

They're still there, doing their duck thing, diving and feeding.

I'm totally focused, like a cat on a mouse, intent on making my first solo kill, a man now, alone in the wild.

A little bit closer and I've got 'em, but they're too wary and their eyesight's too good and in a burst of wings and water they take to the air.

I jump up, shotgun coming to my shoulder, pick out a bird that's separated from the rest of the bunch and is flying around to my left and is going to circle back behind me.

Just as I get a bead drawn on 'em and am pulling out in front of 'em to lead 'em, I glimpse something from the corner of my eye. I instantly recognize it for what it is and some of the "grown man" on his first "solo" hunt in the wild goes out of me with a sigh.

There's my Dad with my little brother Kenny, laying flat on their bellies. Daddy's got his hand over Kenny's head holding him to the ground.

I take my shotgun down, putting the safety on and kinda just stand there watching 'em.

After four or five seconds and no shot, I see Daddy raise his head, see me, and tell brother Kenny he can get up now.

"What ya'll doing, Pop?" I ask walking toward 'em

"We were just kinda checking you out, seeing if you were gonna do o.k." Daddy says.

"What ya'll doing laying on the ground like that?" I ask.

"Well son, you were intent on those birds and when that one broke from the bunch and doubled back behind you…"

I could read his mind. He was worried I might shoot in their direction, so they hit the dirt.

I felt like the twelve year old that I was. A little boy again. Daddy still supervising, watching out for me.

He just loves me, that's all. Wanted to make sure I'm alright. Wanted to watch me "grow up", wanted to be a witness to the first step from boy to man.

"You just go on now son, me and Kenny will walk back to the house," "Be careful and home by dark."

"Yessir, I will."

"Love you son."

"Love you too, Dad."

And the adventure began again.

LITTLE RIVER　　　　　　　CLAY MARSHALL LOVEL　　7-　-99

Little River

When I was in my late 20's, early 30's, we ran out of places to hunt. All the places we'd grown up hunting were private, posted, plantations or public. We had to improvise, so we started taking Bobby's canoe, putting in at the bridge on U.S. 90 and hunting the river swamp that borders the log-filled creek called Little River.

Now all the land was leased out to hunting clubs on both sides of the Little River. The clubs all had game plots and fancy deer stands on the highland. Seldom did any of the members bother going into the river swamp to hunt, and that was fine by us cause we didn't want to share any of their deer and turkey with 'em anyway.

I'm glad we took advantage of that beautiful river swamp when we did. It was loaded with wet weather ponds that were filled with cypress and gum trees. You could ease up to one of those ponds, hide in the brush on the edge of the hardwood hammocks and sit there, being able to look a hundred or a hundred and fifty yards down the pond cause all the underbrush was shaded out by the leaves on the big trees. Sunlight shot in shafts down onto the floor of the forest making deer or turkeys look like they had spotlights on 'em when they'd pass from the shadows into the pools of light.

Those woods are gone now. The hardwood and cypress got too valuable and the weather got too dry for too long, enabling the heavy equipment needed to harvest that timber, to get to it.

We had many an adventure down Little River. Hauled a lot of game, fish and memories out in that ole canoe.

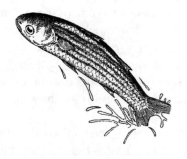

Bobby's Boar and Buck

We did the normal routine that morning. Put the canoe in before daylight, letting the current take us the mile or so we wanted to go before getting out on the west bank at "our place". We'd drag the camoed canoe into some bushes, quietly discuss what time we'd meet back up, and then Bobby and I would go off our separate way to our favorite pond or hammock.

I was sitting quiet and still, watching some does and yearlings eating acorns, when I heard Bobby's 300 Magnum go off. I continued to sit there watching and listening for two minutes or so when I heard Bobby fire again. There's no mistaking that 300 when he shoots, the leaves fall for an hour from the blast. I still don't know why he shoots something that big, but it seems to work well for 'em.

I decided then I better go check it out cause we sorta like to move from that location after we shoot, case someone else comes to check it out too.

Finally located Bobby about 300 yards down river from where I'd sat.

He was excited, eyes wide, out of breath, gestulating wildly as he told me the story, going through the motions with his rifle during the good parts.

A big black boar, well over two hundred pounds as it turns out, had fed up close to Bobby not long after daylight. He'd taken careful aim at his head through the scope and shot 'em. That was the first shot I'd heard.

He'd gotten up from his hiding place, leaned his rifle against the tree the hog was laying by, and got out his knife to cut the hogs throat and let 'em bleed.

He says he bent over the hog and then jerked back up cause it sounded like somebody was driving a bus through the brush, coming straight toward 'em, where there ain't no road.

A big four point comes busting out of the bushes and runs right by 'em, ten feet away.

He grabs his rifle from where it's leaning against the tree and two more bucks with good racks charge by before he can get it up to his shoulder. As the deer disappear into the swamp and he lowers his rifle, a spike and another buck, running together, come charging down the same path as the other three deer had, but he can't find 'em in his scope cause they're so close and going so fast.

He tells me he's about to go nuts at this point. More bucks than he's seen in the past five years have gone by not ten feet away and he can't even get a shot.

Then another deer breaks into the clearing, a big deer, with big horns on his head and he sees Bobby and stops, just for a heartbeat and he wheels around to go the other way, but he stops long enough for Bobby to throw his rifle up and shoot. The deer gets knocked down, jumps up like a jackrabbit and runs outta sight in a split second.

There's a good blood trail heading towards the river. Bobby followed it and lost it and now he's hunting me to come help.

We go back and start following the blood trail from the beginning. You can run and follow it to start with, there's so much. Then there's the occasional splotches of blood, then down to a few drops, then nothing.

We back up to the last few drops of blood we could find. Bobby stays there while I search around in a slow arc in front of 'em, working toward the river all the time.

I finally find some wet blood smeared three feet off the ground on a bush top. The deer's got to be still leaping and bounding through the woods to get sign that high.

Bobby moves up to the new spot.

I move out searching again. I call Bobby to come look at what I'd found. It was a three-inch piece of bright red bone about the size of a twelve-gauge shotgun shell lying on the ground.

We look at each other, thinking the same thing. That 300 Magnum packs a hell of a punch and for that ole buck to be dropping bone he's got to hit hard.

We can't find any more blood sign. It's like he just dried up.

Bobby's holding the place we found the bone and I notice at shoulder height, a freshly skint place on the bark of a medium size oak tree.

Bobby comes up again, I hold the place and he searches up ahead.

He calls me to come on, and I can hear awe and excitement in his voice.

The deer's laying dead at the base of a big hickory tree. Looks like he hit it going wide open. He's a huge eight point, perfect rack, close to two hundred pounds. Bobby's Magnum hit 'em in the hindquarter traveling up through his body. He'd run and jumped through the woods, I guess til he'd pumped all his blood out and had still managed another hundred yards after that. I think he'd run the last fifty yards or so, dead; just on heart and instinct. His horns were full of leaves and there was bark embedded in the rough place on his brow tines from slamming into the trees.

I know he was heavy. We were gasping and soaked with sweat just dragging 'em the hundred yards to the river. We hid 'em in some bushes, rested a few minutes and went back for the hog. He was a good three to four hundred yards from the river and a heap more harder to drag cause he didn't have those convenient handles that buck had, and was heavier to boot.

38

About halfway back to the river, us panting and hassling like sled dogs, we jumped two big spotted hogs that grunted, ran ten yards and stopped.

I had my ought-six on 'em ready to pull the trigger when I realized I'd have to drag them out too. I'd had all the meat dragging I wanted for that day so we let 'em go.

We felt like Hiawatha, Oceola, Crazy Horse and Sitting Bull all wrapped into one that day as we paddled that canoe back up Little River. We had that trophy buck, the two of us, two good rifles and a fat black hog to present the tribe that night.

I can look at the deer's head, mounted on Bobby's wall at his home and recall the Little River, in all its glory in those days.

My Six Point

Same river swamp. Same routine only this particular day its pouring rain in December and it doesn't stop.

I've been up in a fork of a live oak tree about eight feet off the ground. I'm standing on a limb, leaning against the trunk, soaked to the skin for the last two hours.

It's raining so hard that you can't hear anything at all except the rain and you can only see about twenty-five yards before everything grays out from all the water falling from the sky.

I've had it.

I'm cold, wet and starting to shiver. Water's running down my back, down the crack of my ass, in my shoes, my hat's soaked thru, scope's fogged up.

I'm getting down and working my way back to "our place" where we stashed the canoe and hope Bobby's waiting there for me.

The woods are full of water. All the ponds are holding at least a foot and even on the high hammocks there's water standing on the ground. The visibility's so bad I've got to get my compass out to get my bearings to the river. I finally get lined out and go sloshing and slipping through the woods, still looking for a deer, all sound I make drowned out by the rain.

I come around a bend in the dim trail I'm following and there's a big palmetto patch, shiny green against the dark woods in the rain.

Twenty feet away, a buck, (all I see is horns) shoots straight up, like a jack-in-the-box out of the middle of those palmettos. As he's coming down my ole ought-six is coming up to my shoulder, cheek to the stock, finger on the trigger, instinct. When the deer hits the ground he's lost from sight for a split second but I know he's going to leap again for the dark wall of hardwoods shrouded by the rain.

He leaps, I fire.

He disappears again behind the palmettos.

I know he's going to jump again and I'm going to fire again as long as I can see 'em, every time he makes that jump that covers almost twenty feet he's got to get high enough to see over the palmettos.

Where is he?

I've got my rifle snugged up tight, looking under the scope at my iron sights, blinking water from my eyes.

No deer. No sound, except the rain beating on the woods.

I'm standing halfway up to my knees in water, rain pouring off the brim of my hat, running over the top of my rifle. I'm no longer cold, don't feel the wet, tuned in to this instant drama I'm a part of.

41

I can't believe that one shot is all I'm going to get. That one, quick, spontaneous shot that must have come from some ancient ancestor's gene, cause the mind can't think that fast, to raise the gun, punch off the safety, take aim, swing and fire.

I ease around the end of the palmetto patch, gun ready and he's there. He's dead. Shot through the neck and not even twitching. I poke 'em with the barrel of my rifle, but it's over.

I admire his horns, small but a nice six point. I pat his fur down smooth and marvel at their sleek bodies, check his feet for size and shape, lift his head and shoulders guessing his weight.

I try, dragging 'em a little ways myself, thinking I'll have to go find Bobby to help, but there's so much water standing on the ground, that the deer half floats and he's no trouble at all sliding along behind me.

Primordial man in a primordial forest, buck horns in one hand, rifle in the other, dragging his prey home in a driving winter rain storm to eat, drink, brag and strut. To relive the kill over and over again, split second by split second, making one jump and one shot an all nite tale.

Why do we love it so?

Swamp Turkeys

I was slipping my way along to some different territory when I left "our place" that morning.

Three or four steps, stop, look, listen. There was a good dew that nite and the leaves weren't crunchy yet so I was fairly quiet.

I saw movement between some trees, and studied that real hard.

A turkey's head came into view and then it's body, a good sized hen.

I'd passed up a lot of shots at turkeys, wanting to kill a deer, but for some reason I instantly decided I wanted a bird to eat so I raised that ole ought-six up, took a careful bead on the turkey's neck, where it joined the body and pulled the trigger.

With the shot the bird went to flopping on the ground; and all the turkeys in the world went to putting and squawking and flapping and flying everywhere. I'd been so busy looking at that bird on the ground I didn't notice the dozen or more roosted in the trees above 'em.

A gobbler sails out of the trees, going to my left and I automatically raise my rifle and swing to a little open hole in the tree tops. As the bird flies across that opening I follow 'em through it, looking down my iron-sights, lead 'em a little like a dove and fire again. He falls like a rock dropped from a plane and I'm running to pounce on 'em before he can get away.

Ain't no need to hurry, as I soon find out, and I can't believe my eyes. Number one, I've killed 'em with a rifle flying. That's quite a feat in itself, but number two, I've shot that bird's head almost off, attached only by a little piece of neck skin.

Ain't I something. Nobody's going to believe it.

Wait a minute, I've killed another one on the ground before I shot this one, I'm gonna go home with two birds!

I snatch up the one I shot flying and run to where I shot the one standing still on the ground.

No bird. He's got to be here somewhere cause there's enough feathers to stuff a pillow, but no bird.

I search everywhere, looking under every bush and palmetto, wading into every thicket for fifty yards around, but no bird.

I desperately want to walk back into camp with my rifle on my shoulder and a big turkey in each hand but I never find the second one. Must have just grazed 'em cause all I find is feathers, no blood, no bone, no hide.

I don't know if I ever convinced the boys that I'd shot the turkey flying, in the neck and all, but I know I did it. I'll always know I did it. No luck involved what so ever.

43

LITTLE RIVER: CLAY MARSHALL LOVEL

White Water Canoein'

The Little River's usually a lazy little stream. Twenty to twenty five yards wide at it's widest point down to just a few yards in places where the banks are steep. It winds around like a snake, almost doubling back on itself in places, full of dead trees we had to drag the boat over. You can wade across it most anywhere, most the time.

This particular time you couldn't wade across it anywhere.

We'd had one of our famous weeklong winter rainstorms. A front that stalls when it hits the Gulf of Mexico and just sits there and pours rain out.

The rain had finally stopped so we loaded up the faithful canoe and went to the river.

It was in rare form. Normally it's about fifteen feet from the bridge down to the surface of the water. That day there might have been two feet between the water and bridge. It was roaring, literally roaring, foaming and boiling like a big river on its way to the ocean.

We looked at it, pondered on it a few minutes and decided all that water would bunch the deer up for us on some of those higher hammocks we've seen on other trips.

We launch the canoe in the ditch beside the highway, push out into the main stream and away we go, just paddling enough to steer, having all the speed we need provided by the flow of the water.

Two or three bends we go down in no time at all, kind of enjoying the ride with the speed we're making. We're on a straight part of the river when we notice that there's whitewater tearing through what's normally thick woods and that water's really hauling ass even faster than what we're doing.

Bobby and I had seen all the pictures of people shooting the rapids on T.V. and in movies and it sure looked like fun. We never got to travel anywhere that had whitewater canoeing so we real quick-like decided this was our chance to experience it and we weren't going to miss it.

I'm in the front paddling, Bobby's in the back steering. Two quick thrusts with our paddles and we make that white capped water where it's flowing through the woods, cutting the corner of a bend in the river.

That quick, stupid decision we made took us both as close to death by drowning as I hope I'll ever get.

When our canoe went into that racing, roaring water it picked up speed like a high-performance car does when you shift, hard, from second to third. You could feel the acceleration jerk you back in your seat.

We're yahooing, Bobby's trying to steer and I'm using my paddle to push us away from big hardwood trees. At first it was fun and excitement.

Seconds later we're deathly quiet and desperately struggling to keep from being smashed against these big hardwoods that we're being hurled at by the force of the water.

I'm pushing off trees to my left, instantly having to push off on the right, two trees to the left, vines catching our necks and arms, another tree flying up to meet us and finally too many trees to dodge and we can't stop or even slow down.

We smash into one large tree, careen off to the right, hit another one and the force of the water throws us sideways to the current, pushes one side of the boat up the side of the tree and the water pours in the low side of the canoe, instantly filling it. The force of that flooded river is ripping the canoe, now sunk, out from under us.

In a flash I know we can't let the canoe go or we're goners. The main run of the river's only yards away, boiling and churning. If we get swept into that, we're dead. Both of us have on insulated jump suits and already must weigh and extra hundred pounds or more from the water we've soaked up.

Bobby's holding on to a tree at his end of the canoe, I've got ahold of one on my end. I tell Bobby to grab the sunk side of the canoe and pull up while I do the same. With the strength that comes with fear, we manage to raise the low side above water level and the force of the river pins the canoe against the two trees, holding it there.

There we sit. Thankfully pinned, canoe longways against the current. I'm on my knees in the bottom of the canoe, hands full of tree and boat, water up to my waist, Bobby's the same. Limbs, logs and debris are flying by in the floodwaters, bumping the canoe, swirling around to be sucked down and disappear when they pass us and reach the main river channel.

We're in a dangerous situation, trapped like we are, but we've got time to think and reason if we don't panic.

"Just hold on to what you've got", I tell Bobby, which was a stupid statement now that I think about it. If we don't "hold what we've got" we're dead.

We can't climb the trees, they're too big, wet and slippery and we're too heavy.

We damn sure can't try to swim for obvious reasons.

But we can't stay here. The strain of holding the canoe up and holding to the trees is wearing us down.

The high ground bordering the flooded river is about ten yards away from my end of the canoe. An idea comes to my head, but it's going to be a one shot deal and if we miss we'll be in the main river channel.

I tell Bobby that on the count of three, he's to push with all his might off his tree, towards the bank. I'm gonna do the same. I'm hoping the force of the river will push the sunk canoe at an angle close enough that we can reach the bank.

One, two, three.

With yells of strain, exertion and fear we push the canoe forward. We've got to get it past the tree I was holding, to be propelled in the right direction. The current catches the sunk bow of the canoe and angles it downstream. Bobby gives another mighty shove when my tree goes past 'em.

We're picking up speed and we're going to miss the bank by two or three yards. We're still upright but the canoe's starting to roll and I'm staring at the main river channel only yards away.

There's a short piece of rope tied to the bow floating in the water beside me and I grab it and dive out, trying to make the bank. Limbs in my face, vines grabbing my arms, water in my eyes, sodden and sinking. I'm like a threshing machine tearing through the water and brush to reach that bank.

The trees save us again.

My right hand's like a vise grip as it closes around the trunk of a small holly tree, growing out of the water on the edge of safety.

The rope come tight in my left hand as the canoe swings around in the current. Bobby's bailing out of the sunk canoe holding on to it, then the rope, then to me as he scrambles for the bank.

We snatch together on the rope and bring the canoe up close to the dry ground. For two or three full minutes all you can hear is the roar of the river and our heavy, labored breathing as we lie soaking wet on our backs on the ground, thankful to be alive.

We must have set there for an hour or more after we got our composure back.

God, the woods looked beautiful.

God, the river looks powerful, and is.

God, we sure are stupid, but that won't happen again.

We were happy as larks as we dumped the water out of the canoe and rounded up some limbs to push and paddle our way home. You'd think we won the lottery or killed the biggest buck in the world instead of just getting a second chance to live the rest of our lives.

Buck in the Creek

I believe it was in February. We needed mullet at the restaurant and I had come down early that morning to try and catch some.

Fish are scarce that time of year, but usually you can find a few in the creeks where the water's warm. So, I eased my way up Spring Creek to a hole I hoped would pay off.

There was a mist coming off the water that morning, the water being a constant 70 degrees and the air a lot cooler. The mist looked like a multitude of ghosts rising up and drifting down the creek with the breeze. Always attached to the water like they couldn't break away and were bound to it, to disappear forever if they ever broke loose.

Around the third bend in the creek I saw something in the water.

I couldn't quite make out what it was.

I shut off my motor and drifted.

Then, I recognized what I'm looking at.

It was a buck.

A big buck, swimming across the creek, about to make it to the marsh grass on the other side.

Now the rest of this story may seem a little heartless and mean, but it all happened in seconds and it's what happens when the hunter-gatherer instinct takes over, which I've realized over the years fishing and hunting that I have in a strong way.

Can't explain it, just have it. Think everybody had it years and years ago, but it's been civilized out of us.

Back to the story.

I cranked that old 40 horse.

The buck is almost to the bank.

Instinct has taken over and I want that deer.

Twisting the handle on that ole 40 I head the 20 yards to the deer just as he's making his leap to the marsh. Sliding that old mullet skiff through the marsh grass I knock the buck back in the creek with the side of my boat as I spin out back into the creek.

The buck digs off trying to make it back to the marsh, leaping and lunging through the black water of the creek.

I jump off the bottom of the boat where I'd been thrown, grab that motor handle again and point the boat straight at the deer who has gained the edge of the marsh and is one leap away from escape.

Right over the top of that big deer I run my flat bottom boat. The deer lets out a bellow that would have done any prize bull proud, the first time I'd ever heard a deer holler with rage.

Now I've got 'em.

His big ole horny head is right there beside my boat. He's pinned underneath me and he can't get away. All I've got to do is knock 'em in the head with the sash weight I use to strike my nets off.

I reach down, grab the sash weight in one hand, grab a hand full of horns in the other, and stretch way up to knock his brains out with one big blow, when that deer shoots out from under my boat like he was spring loaded. All I hit is air with the sash weight and almost lost an arm when the deer left cause I couldn't turn loose fast enough.

Got snatched out of the boat as it was.

The deer is gone like the mist.

Disappointed, bruised, dirty and breathless I got out in the marsh to try to shove my boat off the hill and back into the water. Finally getting it to float, I decide to go back to the dock, recoup and go fishing later.

When I walk up to the restaurant, Daddy and Puddlebug are standing in the parking lot laughing, with looks of amusement on their faces.

"What's going on?" I ask.

"You won't believe it!" they say.

Daddy proceeds to tell me that he and Puddle are sitting in the restaurant, drinking coffee when they hear all the little yard dogs in Spring Creek yipping and yapping and raising hell in general. They look outside and see this big buck jumping and hopping and running all around the parking lot with all the little dogs in tow, checking 'em out.

Daddy says the deer finally gets straightened out and gallops up the road about 50 yards to Mrs. Coggins' house with all the little dogs still strung out behind 'em. He wheels around, puts his head down and rams Mrs. Coggins' chain link fence, knocking the top railing off and leaving a big dent in her chain link. All the while bucking and snorting and fighting with that little fence.

At this all the little dogs go to squealing and running home to hide under their respective porches and fence rows, real quiet like.

Daddy says the old buck jumped over the fence out of Mrs. Coggins' yard, jumped into the creek and swam across, never to be seen again.

Wonder what got him so riled up?

NOVEMBER RUN SEASON   CLAY MARSHALL LOVEL   7-24-99

November Run Season

I wish you could have seen the crew that gathered up in Goose Creek Bay on that freezing, windy, blue November Sunday morning.

I promise you it wasn't any big church going group.

A twenty-five knot nor'wester was blowing all the water outta the bay and we were waiting for the fish to fall out with it.

The Spears boys, in Lee Allen's big tunnel boat tied-up to chat and Scrunch in his airboat, pulled up too. Then came Samps boat, some of the Panacea crowd in two tunnel boats, the Noe boys in their leaky rig and finally the Nichols crowd.

Everybody was freezing but everybody was excited.

We all had on every bit of clothes we could find. Some of it might not be considered clothing, but anything to break that cold, cold wind.

Some of the boys had oyster sacks around their necks for scarves.

More than one had socks on his hands for gloves.

There were homemade ski masks out of flour sacks, many had on old worn out army jackets. One fella had plastic ice bags over his socks to keep his feet dry cause his boots had holes in 'em.

Fishermen set their own fashion trends when the weather suddenly turns cold.

The boats, rigs and gear that was rafted up that day were a sight to study on too. Scrunch's dark green airboat, twenty-four feet long, five hundred horse Cadillac engine, a thousand yards of net piled on front, held down with a tarp. Lee's big mullet skiff with a one-fifty Evinrude, twelve hundred yards of net like a small plastic mountain stacked up on the net table at the stern. The Panacea boys fished boats I wouldn't use on a bream pond. Boards popped loose and dangling along the rails. Motors that ran on one cylinder, if they ran at all. Boats that leaked so bad that somebody had to be constantly bailing water out to keep 'em from sinking right there, but they'd have a load of ragged-out gill net to strike the fish with.

The Nichols boys always had good rigs. Bow rails bolted on the tip of the bow cap so they could stand up high and look down in the water to spot the fish. New one-fifteen Yamahas, nice paint jobs and glass work, a thousand, fifteen hundred yards of net, neatly stacked ready to strike.

Me in my ole mullet skiff, forty horse Yamaha, nineteen-foot wooden boat with six hundred yards of net and an ice box for five hundred pounds.

This was a wild, excited, wound-up rough looking bunch all tied up in a wad drifting through Goose Creek Bay.

Two or three pints of dark whiskey came out of some of those old fatigue jackets. They were readily passed hand to hand, boat to boat, almost everybody taking an early morning slug just to be sociable. That whiskey burned like fire when it went down, to be chased by coffee if you had it. It felt good though, a contrast to the freezing ears and numb toes.

I think that whiskey was like a mullet fishermen's communion, with most everybody partaking, whether they wanted a drink or not, just to show that for that moment, everybody was together, almost friends, cause this was a collection of loners, competitors, people that didn't get along with each other all the time.

Everybody knew that the fish had left the river the night before and had gone in to Sheppard Springs and Graves Creek and they were going to have to come out with this tide.

There was a payday coming if the boat didn't tear up and you could stand the weather.

We stayed ganged-up joking and throwing insults until the first shake of fish showed up, coming by Nat's Point. They were jammed up, in a tight ball in water too shallow for a pelican to dive on 'em and none of us, especially me, can stand to let a good bunch of mullet go by, so the flotilla of flour sacked and oyster-bagged fishermen broke up.

One leaving, then two.

Everybody going after their own bunch of fish in their own special places. Hoping that the bunch they struck would be the Mother Lode, with all the red roe in it. Everybody caught up in the spirit of the chase, the hunt, the cold, the wind, the thrill of trying to be in the right place at the right time to harvest a small amount of one of the greatest crops in the world, Mother Nature crops. Fish.

Mullet in particular, that only she can plant, nurture and grow and will always continue to give us to harvest as long as man himself does not interfere with pollution and destruction of habitat.

THE TURNER HOUSE BURNS   CLAY MARSHALL LOVEL   6-9-99

The Turner House Burns

Curt and Bort-Lee lived with their mama, Flonza, about a block from the restaurant.

At first glance you'd think that Curt and Bort were young boys, riding their bikes around Spring Creek, until you noticed they were drinking Budweiser beer and both had full beards.

Curt and Bort were kind of strange. I never did quite figure them out but they never worked, drank a lot and fished a lot, kind of quiet too.

One Sunday morning their house burnt down. We heard that Curt had decided to fry some fish he'd caught the day before. He had put some grease on the stove to heat up, sat down in his easy chair and sort of passed out, from all his bike riding and beer drinking.

Lucky for him the sounds of the flames woke 'em up and he ran out and hid in the bushes behind the house, knowing he was going to catch hell for setting the house on fire.

Somebody in town spotted the flames and called the volunteer fire department and also called Curt and Bort's older brother Terrel, who lives in Woodville and told 'em about the fire.

When Terrel arrives, the house is almost totally engulfed in flames. Bort-Lee, Curt's older brother, is standing in the doorway dressed in his year long uniform (even though it's 100 degrees in July) of a heavy leather flight jacket, zipped up with a fur collar, jeans and a wool stocking cap.

Bort is calmly standing in the doorway, even though the door frame is totally on fire, eating a can of cold pork and beans with a spoon, watching the fire burn the wood around him as if it's just a TV show.

Terrel, concerned for his mother and brother who are unaccounted for, (Flonza is at a neighbor's and remember Curt is still hiding in the bushes) runs up on the porch with Bort and yells "Bort, where's Mom and Curt?"

"Go to hell you suma bitch," replies Bort between mouthfuls of cold pork and beans.

"Where's Curt and Mama?" yells Terrel over the flames.

"Go to hell you suma bitch," replies Bort again, shoveling his mouth full of beans.

Terrel tries to look in the window from the front porch to see if anyone is in the house and the heat explodes the glass in the window knocking Terrel off the porch and onto the ground.

As Terrel is picking himself up off the ground he spies an old round point shovel laying there and begins to jump up and down on the shovel handle until he breaks the handle out. Picking the handle up he turns to

Bort, who is still eating his pork and beans and yells, "I've always wanted to beat your ass and now I'm gonna do it."

So now with the house totally engulfed in flames, shooting fire 40 feet in the air, all the residents of Spring Creek watching, the Volunteer fire department setting up to battle the blaze, Terrel drags Bort-Lee off the porch and proceeds to put that old shovel handle to good use, not fighting the fire as most would think, but holding Bort by the collar of his old flight jacket and beating the hell out of 'em in the yard. While the house burns down to the ground.

Nobody tried to stop Terrel until they though Bort-Lee had had a good beating, that most thought he deserved.

Just A Day A the Office

I was unloading my boat at dusk dark. I'd been out scrapping up Roe Mullet, looking for a big bunch. Hadn't found it.

Lee Nell was standing on the dock, telling Bruce and Lee where he would be, to catch a buncha fish, if he was still fishing.

They were paying close attention and so was I cause Mr. Lee Nell had caught more mullet in his lifetime than all three of us together would ever hope to see.

He was telling 'em to be at the Goose Creek Seinyard well before daylight. Not at daylight, but in the black dark before daylight. There was a front coming thru and he knew where the fish were gonna move. He knew exactly where and when that big bunch of run mullet were gonna go and I can testify to it.

I was late the next morning; not real late but too late.

I didn't make it to my skiff til about six thirty the next morning. I was running wide open headed for Goose Creek, picturing that huge run of fish coming down the shoreline when I spied Lee Allen's boat, slowly plowing along, rising sun still attached to the water, already coming back.

Just the bow caps of the boat's sticking up outta the water. Lee and Bruce motioning us with their arms to slow down, don't throw any wake or it'll swamp their boats.

They're loaded.

Both boat's loaded so heavy with fish that they're flush with the level of the water in the bay, just the forward movement of the boat keeping 'em from sinking.

They had just over six thousand pounds as it turned out. Bruce not even putting his net overboard cause they knew they couldn't haul anymore than Lee Allen was catching in his net.

Mr. Lee Nell had been right and I'd been late but the sun was just coming up and I was determined to find the rest of that bunch, or another one. I took off to the east searching and looking, mad at myself for missing out on that big lick.

All Goose Creek Bay I searched, no fish. Up Sheppard Springs, Gander Creek, Mentzler, Graves, no fish.

I finally anchored down 'bout mid morning, at the mouth of Sheppard Springs to wait and hope another bunch would try to slip by in the channel.

I was disgusted, and Mark, my brother-in-law who was fishing with me, wasn't real happy either. We both needed the money and our pride had a big bruise on it too.

I'm ready to go somewhere. Anywhere where there's some fish. I'm

59

tired of waiting on 'em, not being too patient anyway.

"Let's go", I tell Mark. He's bent over in the bottom of the boat, bailing water out from a leak we'd sprung, slamming into an oyster bar.

I reach over the bow and grab the anchor rope. Bent over and facing down at the water my eyes about pop outta my head.

The whole bottom, four feet under the boat is moving black with mullet. They're packed up in a solid stream, bellies touching the sand, moving quiet but steady, sneaking by the boat.

"Throw it out", I yell, snatching the anchor.

"What?" Marks says, still bailing water.

"Pitch out the staff, now!" I shout as I'm jerking the crank cord on my ole forty horse.

Mark stands up and looks at me like I'm crazy but does what I said. I twist the throttle wide open and steer the boat in a hard turn.

Mark's trying to keep from being thrown out as the net peels off the back of the boat.

Fish are going in the air, jumping the net as I close the circle and start to wind 'em down. They really put on a show as the circles get smaller and tighter.

Mark and I are stunned but happy as we go from mad to glad in thirty seconds.

No fish, no money one minute. Fish and money the next, in the blink of an eye.

We fill the fish box. Somewhere between five and six hundred pounds. We start putting 'em in the floor of the boat, the net's only half cleared.

We're happy when we get cleared up. The box is full. We're knee deep in fish, standing on the deck. Fish flipping and flopping, throwing water and scales on us, almost swimming in the bottom of that old leaky boat. We don't care, we like fish juice on us, that ole musty run mullet smell. Smells like money to us.

We're heading home now, not making quick time cause of the load we're toting. Over a thousand pounds of red and white roe mullet. We're just off the old seinyard when I look up toward Nats Point and see a boat pitch out his staff and make that familiar big circle, penning fish.

I shut the motor off, looking at the shoreline, seeing if there's another bunch we can put our net around. You can't ever catch too many.

We're sitting there looking, when the boat that's striking fish below us, gets through winding 'em down and shuts off.

It's slick calm and pretty. You can hear every sound on the water when it's like that. We can hear the last corks coming off Curtis' boat, bumping over the stern as he glides to a stop, must be a half mile away. We can hear his oar bumping on the side of the boat as he straightens it up to start taking up his net.

We can really hear good the sound of Curtis' voice as he shouts at the top of his lungs.

"You no good son of a biiiitch."

"I'm gonna stomp your ass as soon as I get this net up for stopping in front of me and cutting me off!"

Me and Mark laugh knowing Curtis must be messing with us cause we're sure he recognizes our boat, we sure recognize his.

"You sorry bastard, wait til I get my hands on you", echoes down the bay, the madness plain in the tone of his voice.

I had just gone from sad to glad with our good catch of fish, now I'm going from glad to mad real fast.

Curtis is still yelling and cussing us, and I'm going to find out why.

I crank that ole forty horse and head in a beeline to Curtis' boat throwing a big wake and bogging down from the weight of the fish.

We get up close to Curtis' boat, shut off, and I ask Curtis what's going on.

He starts cussing me, threatening me, telling me what he's gonna do to me soon as he can get his net up.

J.T., Curtis' deckhand was steady taking up net, never looking at me, staring straight ahead, nervous, saying nothing.

Curtis gets his breath from cussing me and starts up again.

That does it.

I pop my cork, and I ain't a pretty sight.

Jumping to the back of the boat, I snatch the "staff", really a six pound iron sash weight, from Mark's hand, who's been holding it, case we struck some fish. Hopping back to the motor I crank it and run the ten yards separating the two boats, til they touch. Standing on the bow cap, sash weight in my hand, vein-popping mad, I start telling Curtis a few things at the top of my lungs.

I tell 'em to come on.

I tell 'em how fat he is.

I talk about his ancestry.

I tell 'em I'm going to kill 'em.

I tell 'em what a sorry fisherman he is.

I tell 'em about the load of fish I've already got.

I tell 'em how fat he is again!

I tell 'em to come on right now, I want to knock his brains out.

I go on and on and on raging on the bow cap like a mad monkey. Finally, I run out of things to say and breath.

It's quiet.

The boats are drifting apart now cause Curtis and J.T. have been steady taking up net during my tirade.

Curtis throws out an "I'll get you later" but it don't sound real serious.

I reply with, "You know where to find me" and crank my boat.

I think Curtis was probably thinking about his weight problem with all the descriptions of what a fat so and so, and what fat such and such I'd described 'em as. Anyway, the fire seemed to be gone.

My fire was about out too. I was tired from cussing.

We hit another small lick of fish on the way in, giving us almost twelve hundred pounds for the morning. Redeeming ourselves a little for being late to work that day.

Just another day at the office.

The Turn-Back Side

We talk about mullet fishing a lot cause we used to do so much of it. In doing so much of it we get to observe the habits of the fish, where they went, what they did.

I can tell ya what they do when they're running down the shoreline in good-sized bunches during the fall and winter.

I can tell ya what they do when you spook 'em, when you go try putting that net around 'em.

They turn back,

They turn back, in mass, with the mullet in front of the school piling on top of the ones that hadn't turned around yet. In a split second they all get turned around swimming full speed, packed up, going back in the direction they came from.

You got to have that net in front of 'em, cutting 'em off, if you don't you won't catch any fish.

That's the "Turn Back Side".

If you do get the net struck off in time on the turn back side, get ready to try to get more net off to back-up what you already got out cause the fish are going to stomp it down. Sink it. Carry the cork line to the bottom when that panicked ball of fish hits the net. When the head of the bunch first hits the net they fill every mesh in the net and the weight of the fish behind 'em flatten it, letting most the fish get out.

I always tried to be pouring more net to 'em in the direction of the turn back side, striking the net in big curly-cues, letting 'em sink one piece and run into another.

Let 'em sink it.

When none of the corks are showing and ya got two or three laps of curly-cued net struck off, ya know you got 'em.

Rope 'em on.

Clear 'em out.

Get ready for the next bunch.

You know after I got to noticing that the mullet "turn back" when they're scared or startled, I also get to noticing that most animals "turn back". Notice the next possum or deer that you spook on the road or in the woods. It may be a natural reaction of most critters, fish, game and people to "turn back".

I guess the way they came from was safe when they went by and they're going back to that safe place.

Well the "turn back side" ain't always the safe way to go, not if I can get my net there first.

GATORS   CLAY MARSHALL LOVEL   6-11-99

Gators

Being born and raised in the south, on the water or around it all the time, we've met our share of gators. Most the time they don't fool with us and we don't mess with them, but thirty years of being in the gators environment we've learned there are exceptions. Sometimes it seems we just can't help messing with each other.

Here's a few good gator stories.

We've raised little tiny gators in aquariums at the house. Poured tadpoles and baby crawfish in to feed 'em. Watched the cute little gators let the tadpoles and crawfish set on their heads and hide between their legs all day long like all of 'em were best friends.

Until it got dark.

Then it sounded like a feeding frenzy of sharks, all the splashing and chomping and crunching of the little critters that the gator was eating. You'd go in the next morning and there wouldn't be a thing in the tank except the cute gator and few crawfish legs he'd bit off and forgot to eat.

We've served live gator in the restaurant.

What I mean by that is, we've had long, lingering, slightly intoxicated customers that we've needed to gently move along so we could go home, so we've done things like this.

"Wally, would you like to try some fresh gator meat?"

He responds in a slow, relaxed, two-drinks-too-many southern drawl.

"Well, I'm pretty full but I always like fresh gator meat, bring us a little bit."

"Coming right up", I say as I go around the corner, pick up a wax fish box and dump a three foot mad, hissing, snapping, running gator on the floor and he proceeds to run under the lingering party's table.

"Didn't want it quite that fresh", Wally chuckles as he grabs his bottle of scotch in one hand, his screaming wife in the other and follows the rest of the party of six that's hollering, yelling and laughing and charging out the front door.

Now we can clean up and go home, it's been a long day.

We've counted coup on bunches of gators, letting the boys poke 'em with a push pole as the gator thought he was hiding on the bottom. We've done this since the boys were five or six and they're twenty-six and twenty-one now. We still do it on occasion, just to let the gators know that we love 'em.

We've eaten all the gator we've wanted to. Not my favorite meat in the world, kinda like chewy chicken and frog legs mixed.

We've caught 'em in gillnets, seines, cast nets, rod and reels, cane poles, by hand, bullet and spears. Ninety-nine percent of the time we just try to cut 'em loose cause big ones can tear up lots of our gear and the only reason we caught most of 'em was because we didn't see 'em when we'd strike our nets for fish.

Gators cause a lot of their own problems with us, stealing fish out of our nets and bait out of our crab traps, ruining the nets and the traps in the process.

One of my best friends, J.R., who was a paddleboat fisherman before the net ban, had problems with gators. The gators in Walker Creek got familiar with the sound of J.R.'s net being struck off the boat, the corks going bump, bump, bump as they passed over the stern bulkhead. They would come out of the marsh grass while Johnny was still rowing his net out and as soon as the mullet started hitting the net the ole gator would swim over to the fish and eat net and all, evidently thinking that the monofilament netting was a good condiment to go along with his fresh fish, sometimes eating a cork or two for dessert.

Johnny'd get mad, them tearing up his handmade nets like that and stealing his fish that he needed to sell.

He'd try to chase 'em down and beat 'em with his oars but he couldn't catch 'em in that rowboat. God protect the poor old gator that gets fouled in J.R.'s nets. When they do he'll beat 'em til the gator gets out, the oar breaks or the gator's dead, whichever comes first.

I remember one September afternoon J.R. and I were fishing together in separate paddleboats up Walker Creek. Johnny had put a little four horse Johnson on his paddle skiff to help him move from bay to bay without rowing the whole time. His old wooden paddle skiff would go about five miles an hour wide open with that four on it.

I was ahead of Johnny coming down the creek and spied one of the big gators, 'bout a ten-footer, that had been raisin hell with Johnny's nets. He was laying on the edge of a little white sand bar where Redfish Creek turns off, taking a nap and trying to digest his diet of Johnny's mullet and monofilament he'd eaten the night before.

I went right on by the dozing gator, knowing Johnny'd see 'em.

I looked back to watch J.R.'s reaction, I knew he hated that critter.

He'd seen 'em alright. He'd got his little four-horse motor all lined up just right, so his boat would pass close to the gator without him stirring. He was standing up in the middle of the boat getting the heft and balance on his trusty flounder gig, a heavy cypress pole with three hard, steel spear points.

He looked like a madman, with his hat off, thick gray-black hair and mustache blowing in the wind, hateful grimace on his face, spear poised and ready, arm drawn back, full length, to put all the power of his arms and body in the throw. Strength built by twenty-five years of rowing boats and dragging down nets.

I'm watching and the gator's still dozing as an Indian from the past comes charging down the creek in his simple wooded craft and at the precise moment, to use not only his body's thrust but the weight of the boat's thrust also. Johnny takes his revenge. The spear sticking that gator right behind his head.

The water explodes, spray flying, that gator's snapping and growling, J.R.'s screaming like a wild Indian, trying to stay in his boat as the gator thrashes and writhes and boils beneath it.

Johnny knew he couldn't kill that gator with that flounder gig, throwing it like that, but he wanted that gator to know who he was stealing from.

The gig pulled loose, that gator swam off.

Johnny got his spear back and seemed in a better mood the rest of the day.

We got a good laugh on Daddy one time.

Our neighbors, on the next canal had a big gator, 'bout twelve feet, that had lived there for years, but them being new in Spring Creek, they wanted him gone.

Our local trapper, Houston, and his helper Sam-Jack set a big hook with a rope tied to an inner tube, tied to the dock and baited with a chicken.

The next morning the gator took the bait, hooked himself, fought that inner-tube til he was tired.

Somebody heard 'em thrashing around, called Houston and Sam-Jack. They came over and shot 'em between the eyes with a 30:06, hooked a rope to 'em and drug 'em up the boat ramp with their pick-up truck.

The problem was they couldn't load 'em by themselves, cause like I said he was twelve feet long and solid five hundred and fifty pounds.

They came and got us to help. Me, Hubert, Bruce, Jeff and Daddy.

We went over to the next canal and oohed and aaahed over that big gator. His width and length, the size of his head and teeth, his missing right front foot that had long ago been bit off by a really big gator, probably during mating season.

The size of the hole that ought-six made in his hard ole head was pretty impressive too.

Anyway, time to load 'em up, or try to.

Sam-Jacks in the truck with a rope around the gator's head, lifting and pulling, Jeff's got a right front foot, Bruce's got the left. I got the left hind leg, Daddy's got the right. Houston's in the middle and back, lifting for all he's got.

We're all in a bind and a strain, barely getting that gator off the ground, grunting, groaning, cussing, lifting for all we have when that gator decides his right back leg ain't dead yet and he starts jerkin it back and forth.

Well, we're all kinda nervous around this big, bloody, toothy lizard and when he starts twitching his leg and Daddy hollers like he's been snake bit and takes off, it's a lightning-fast, contagious case of the scream and haul-ass that infects us all.

I'm gone, with a loud shout as I vacate the premises.

Jeff and Bruce are turning loose quick with unrecognizable nor understandable sounds leaving their mouths. Poor ole Houston, in the back, almost gets squashed as that five hundred and fifty pounds of dead weight gator comes sliding down on 'em and Sam-Jack is just drug right out the back of the truck still holding that rope attached to the gator's head.

Boy did we laugh, not only at Daddy but at each other too, for running from that ole dead gator and spilling 'em out of the truck that way.

When we finally did get 'em loaded in that old GMC pick-up, I looked at his massive head one more time.

It looked like a toothy smile on his face to me.

Another gator tale comes from Myron's Sinkhole that's located in front of his house.

Bruce (Myron's brother) and I were working on Bruce's new house putting stain on the outside, when we heard Sherry, Myron's wife, go to screaming and hollering.

Bruce and I took off through the woods to see what was going on.

When we got to Myron's house, Sherry and the kids were standing in the front yard all worried looking and pale. They said that Smokey, their Labrador retriever, had come down to the sinkhole where Sherry and the kids were fishing. Smokey went into the bushes, mostly sparkle berry and swamp murtyl, to check something out and they heard a big thrashing sound, one "yip" from the dog, a giant splash, then quiet.

They'd called and called for Smokey but no sign of the dog; just a lot of scratched up leaves and few broken twigs where there'd been some kind of tussle.

It didn't take Bruce and me long to figure out that ole Smokey was gator meat and Smokey was a big, seventy-pound dog.

There wasn't any sign of Smokey or the gator in that limestone sink. That's not unusual, cause big gators carry their prey, after they've drowned 'em, and stuff 'em up in underwater roots or caves to let 'em "tenderize" for a day or two.

We told Sherry the news and she called Houston and Sam-Jack, the trappers, to come catch that mean ass gator that ate Smokey.

Bruce and I stopped by the sinkhole two days later to check on the trapper's progress.

Smokey was floating at the far end of the sink, bloated up and chewed on, he'd broken loose from his underwater food storage locker and was just a bobbin around like a cork.

Sam-Jack was sitting in good rifle shot of that dead dog with his good ole thirty-ought-six, waiting for the gator to come and get a snack.

He didn't get that gator while we were there, but he's patient. He shot 'em the next day, staying on the job the whole time til the gator showed up.

It took a backhoe to load 'em up on Sam-Jack's truck after Sam-Jack had to dive down in the sinkhole to tie a rope to that gator to pull 'em out.

Twelve feet, six inches, six hundred pounds.

I damn sure wouldn't dive in that dark water with that animal no matter how dead he was or supposed to be.

Old Smokey had been caught just by the end of his tail in that gator's mouth and drug into the water. That's all the gator's got to do is get a good grip anywhere and get you in the water, cause then the gator starts to spin and spin and spin and spin, round and round underwater til whatever he's got ahold of quits struggling.

Gators are born with that spinning instinct. You can take the smallest little gator, (I've done it many times) pop a rag at his face til he gets mad and snapping and then let 'em sink his teeth into the rag, pick 'em up off the ground and watch.

Round and round he'll go, staying parallel with the ground, spinning like an overturned wagon wheel from that twisting motion they do with their bodies.

Did you know gators don't swallow food with their heads underwater?

If you watch 'em when they eat, they stick their head straight up out of the water to chew and crunch and swallow their food.

They'll beat the fenders off your truck and bite your tires if you park on the end of their tails.

They'll total out a 1989 Ford Granada if you run over great big ones at night lying in the middle of the road.

They'll scare the hell out of you when they get their teeth hung in your mullet net and elect not to struggle until you've drug 'em up on the net table and all you can see and hear is white mouth and popping jaws as you grab an oar and fight.

Gators are easy to kill if you can catch 'em lying and hidden on the bottom in clear water. All you need is a long pole no bigger around than a broom handle. You idle your boat over the top of the hiding gator, take that pole and poke the gator with the end of it, on top of his head as hard as you can. He'll move about five feet, you line up on 'em and do it again. It might take three times, maybe four, but then you've got a dead gator. You've jarred his little dinosaur brain loose in his head and he's had it.

Gator meat anyone?

Gators are funny critters.

Sometimes they mess with you, sometimes they don't.

We're funny critters, too.

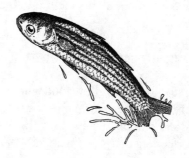

Hubert's at the Hospital

Hubert Hinton is an amazing man. Back in the early 60's he worked for a Georgia Power Company as a lineman. He had a terrible accident that electrocuted 'em and as a result he lost one arm at the shoulder and one leg at the hip.

This didn't seem to slow him down too much. Sometime in the late 70's he came down and leased Spring Creek Marina from us and operated it, doing more work than most people with all their limbs. His wife, Miss Lib, worked hard at his side and between the two of 'em there wasn't anything they couldn't do.

This story is about one of the times Miss Lib went out of town.

Hubert tended to have a few beers every afternoon and evening. When Miss Lib's around he kind of kept his consumption down to a reasonable level, but when she went out of town, he tended to have a few more than usual, visiting with his friends. Late on a Saturday night he decided to climb the three steps up to his front porch, go in his house and go to bed but he didn't quite make it.

Somehow he slipped on the second step, fell over backwards pinching a nerve in his neck and couldn't get up. He laid there hollering and yelling til one of the local fishermen came in from mullet fishing, heard 'em and carried 'em to the hospital.

They called me at home early Sunday morning to pick 'em up and bring 'em home to Spring Creek.

When I arrived at the hospital I could hear Hubert, moaning in pain from the lobby of the emergency room. I found him slumped in a wheel chair doped up with pain medicine, hung over and miserable. He had on a white tee shirt with his big, brown, strong, good arm lying in his lap, the other sleeve was hanging empty. He had a light blue hospital blanket over his one good leg. His wooden leg, complete with boot attached, was laying on a nearby table with his pants still on the false leg, belt and all.

The orderly told me I could take 'em home, gave me some more medicine for 'em, pointed toward the lobby and left.

Hubert's looking, feeling and sounding really bad. He's really out of it with all the medicine they'd given 'em, slumped over, continually making long drawn out moans and groans, almost unconscious.

I'm having trouble myself.

I've got to push the wheelchair and try to carry Hubert's leg at the same time. The only way I can manage is to wrap the empty pants leg around the wooden leg, get his belt around all of it to keep it from unwrapping, balance the false leg on my shoulder with the boot toe pointed down

71

and out in front of me. I wrap my left arm around the thigh part of Hubert's wooden leg to keep it from falling, grab the wheelchair with my right hand and here we go.

The double doors from the emergency ward open. Hubert's moaning with pain, I'm struggling to push the wheelchair. Hubert's leg, boot bobbing up and down, is balanced on my shoulder.

We enter the lobby area waiting room of the hospital.

It's full of ill or injured people and their families.

All talking stops.

All eyes stare and bulge.

Jaws drop.

It's dead silence and we're the center of attention.

I give a little grimace type smile to everyone, nod my head and continue struggling with the wheelchair, trying not to drop Hubert's leg-in-the-pants, all the while Hubert's moaning and groaning real loud.

I could read most people's minds as we rolled through the parking lot.

"They're sending him home?"

"They're sending his leg home separate?"

"Where's his other arm?"

"They're sending him home in that shape?"

"You hear how loud he's moaning and they're sending him home?"

As I was putting Hubert in my truck (his leg had to ride in the back), I noticed that some of the people waiting for service in the emergency room were leaving, glancing over at us as they got in their cars. I guess they decided they felt better or maybe they didn't want to be doctored on at this hospital, specially if they send some of their patients home in pieces, limbs unattached. Maybe seeing Hubert made 'em decide they just weren't feeling "that bad" or maybe it made 'em well or maybe they just decided they'd try another hospital.

CRAZY GEORGE   CLAY MARSHALL LOVEL

Crazy George

I'm mullet fishing again. It's cold, wet and gray, not much wind. The rain came and went and came again. There was a cold front coming through.

I was sitting at the Old Creek Run Stand waiting for a bunch of fish to come by. I'd run all the creeks out and hadn't located anything, so I thought I'd just sit and maybe they'd come to me. The fish tend to lay quiet in the deep channels til everything gets just right and then they'll make their move, sometimes appearing like magic.

What appeared from around the bend, instead of fish, was a boat. A boat like you don't see much anymore, what we call a paddle skiff or a push boat, cause that's what you do. You stand up in it with a nine-foot oar in each hand, facing forward and push it.

I knew who it was, pushing that boat down the creek, it was Crazy George.

Crazy George is one of those people who just appear in small coastal villages. You don't know where they come from, they don't offer to tell you, they're broke, hungry, and will deckhand for a place to live and cigarette money.

Crazy George was one of those people.

Everybody knew 'em, he worked for Doodlebug at the fish house, crewed on one of his boats with Jim and was the only person around that fished a paddle skiff all over the bay.

Miles and miles he pushed those oars, no motor on the boat at all, the only thing on the boat besides George was about four hundred yards of pocket net.

He was built like a professional body builder, huge arms and shoulders, flat hard belly, small waist, bulging thighs and calves. Reddish blond hair and beard, square jaw, piercing, vacant blue eyes. He'd split wood for fun in July, no shirt, muscles rippling, sweat drenched. He'd show off to the young girls, splitting oak logs with one hand, picking up huge, two hundred pound logs over his head. There's not much entertainment down here, it's easy to draw a crowd.

Nobody wanted to mess with George, he wasn't wrapped too tight, sometimes he would throw fits, and looked like he could tear arms off if he wanted to.

The day I saw 'em, he had that old paddle skiff moving. Every push of the oars would make that boat jump. With those big arms and legs behind it, he could take those oars and with every push lift the bow out of the water.

That's what he was doing as I watched 'em. He was getting it on with those oars, you could hear him "whoof" with the effort every time he'd push.

He "whoofed" and pushed to within seventy-five yards of where I was, wheeled his boat around, backed it up to the marsh grass, pitched the end of his net out and settled in to wait for the fish to come down.

He had cut me off from the fish.

He'd set up dead ahead of me, with me in plain sight, and just cut me off, breaking one of the main unwritten rules of mullet fishing. You just don't do that, unless you want trouble.

I'd never had any problems with Crazy George, knew him fairly well, he ordered hamburgers to-go most every night the restaurant was open. Always acted a little crazy, hence the name. If he'd been drinking he'd be a little more crazy, telling outrageous lies and expecting you to believe 'em. We'd just pacify 'em, get 'em his burgers and send him on his way as quick as we could. But I couldn't let this go. Him cutting me off like that, so I fired up my ole forty horse, picked up my net end and idled down to 'em.

He was just sitting there, back toward me, slicker hood pulled over his head to keep the rain off, facing up the creek, looking like a big professional wrestler Viking, waiting on some fish.

"George, didn't you see me sitting back there?"

"Yeah, I saw you, you're in the wrong place," he says.

"George, that's where I want to be and you shouldn't cut me off like that."

"Move down here," he says, still staring up the creek, not moving or looking at me.

"I've got to go to work anyway," I say, "You can have it, but don't cut me off any more."

No response, no nothing; well he's Crazy George, what do you expect.

I crank my motor, idling off up Old Creek, past George, heading back toward the cut-off to Spring Creek, looking for mullet in the light sprinkling rain.

I get about five hundred yards above where George is, and through the drizzle and the fog see the bright silver flash of a mullet as he flips out of the water landing on his side, and flips again like mullet do when they're crowded up tight and get squeezed in the school and just squirt out of the water sideways to get more room.

Another fish flipped.

I shut the motor off to study 'em, to see if there was anything to 'em, to see if I wanted to put my six hundred yards of gill net to 'em in the channel.

Through the fog and the rain I hear in a big booming roar, George cussing me, for a no good son of a bitch for cutting my motor off and getting ahead of 'em. Telling me in no uncertain terms that if I'll come back he'll stomp my ass on the spot.

Nonstop, George keeps cussing, threatening, raising hell. The more he hollered the madder I got.

I knew I ought to just crank up, forget George's bullshit back there and go on to the house, but I couldn't. Crazy George is the one that had cut me off! I'd just stopped in the channel to look at some fish.

I fire up my forty horse, spin the boat around and run, wide open back down Old Creek to where Crazy George is.

George is on the shore. Stomping back and forth, raging, yelling and shaking his fist at me, marching up and down in the marsh grass like a mad bull.

I shut my motor off, staying about ten yards from the end of his boat, in the edge of the channel.

"What the hell is wrong with you George?"

"You got ahead of me," he shouts.

"You tried to cut me off," he yells still stomping, charging up and down in the grass.

"Get out and come up here, I'm going to stomp your ass right now," as he rips off his slicker jacket popping all the buttons off and throws it at me, still stomping back and forth.

"You go to hell, George," I'm not crawling out on that bank with you.

"Your mom and dad," George says "they're alright," he says, "but you, you're, you're, you're, you're a uh, uh (hunting for the right words I guess), you're a bitch." "A bitch is what you are and if you won't come up here I'm coming to get you."

It's raining, it's cold, Crazy George really looks wild and crazy with his long hair all wet and askew. Shirt off, red faced and growling like a bear he comes charging out into the water to get me.

The water goes over his knees, then up to his waist as he lunges through it toward me, arms swing side-to-side, fists clenched.

"Don't come out here George," I say as I pick up my well-worn nine-foot ash oar that Uncle Floyd made for me years ago. "I'll have to kill you if you lay a hand on this boat."

George is out to the boat now, up to his arm pits in the water, staring up at me with those mad blue eyes, taking in that oar that I'm holding like a giant baseball bat.

"You think I'm scared of that oar?" George yells up at me, just his head sticking outta the water now, "we'll see, we'll see," he's yelling as he half swims, half runs, out of the water back to his boat.

He leans on the side of that paddle skiff, dragging around under the bow cap, throwing out his life jacket, his water bottle, whatever junk that was there going in every direction as he frantically searches for something.

"Ah ha," he says triumphantly as he came up with a two foot club, shakes it at me and comes charging back, up to his knees again, to his waist, chest deep, club waving.

"You think I'm scared now," he yells as he reaches the boat.

I can't help it, I try to, but I can't help starting to laugh. I've got my oar stuck straight down in the water, leaning on it, holding the boat from drifting off, looking straight down at Crazy George's head, and that short club sticking up outta the water.

This whole crazy scene just got me, I'm laughing and it's driving Crazy George crazier. I'm trying to tell him to back off or I'm going to have to hurt 'em and laughing at the same time.

"You still think I'm scared," George shouts, "I'll show you," he says as he swings that club with all his immense strength against my oar.

"Crack" goes the club, breaking off even with George's hand, the long end flying off into the channel.

George looks at his hand, opens it and lets the two-inch piece of club, that still remains there, to fall into the water.

"I still ain't scared," he says, but he's backing up toward the shore, glaring at me, but realizing he was in a bad position, me in my boat with that stout oar, and him up to his neck in the water. He's crazy alright but not that crazy.

He begins to stomp up and down the shore again yelling, "I'll get you yet, you bitch you. I'll get you, I'll get you," charging back and forth in a now well-worn path he's flattened in the marsh grass.

"Steer clear of me, George," I say, laughing no longer, realizing how crazy George truly was, unstable.

I left him there in the cold and rain, still pacing back and forth, muttering, yelling stewing in his own juice.

I was a little concerned about how he might act later when I ran into 'em again, as I knew I would, Spring Creek being so small, only about fifty residents.

As I took a shower and got dressed to go to work in the restaurant, I made a hard-thought decision.

I carried a little .25 caliber Luger automatic, that my grandfather had given me, kept it handy in my truck, figured I'd start keeping it in my jacket. I had no intentions of going head to head with Crazy George. I'm no weakling and I'm sure no coward but I don't think you could hurt George hitting 'em over the head with a frying pan, much less hurt him with a fist.

The more I though about it, the more I decided that .25 wasn't big enough. I hoped I'd never have to pull it, but if I did I wanted something to stop 'em.

I got out an old .38 Smith and Wesson I kept in a drawer and put it in my coat pocket, just in case.

Two days went by. Didn't see Crazy George at all, which was alright with me, didn't want to see 'em.

The third night after the incident, the fish decided to run and I went to the Junior store to get some gas for my boat. It was cold and I had my old down-filled fishing jacket, had that .38 in my pocket too.

It was about midnight when I jumped out of the truck at the gas pumps, filled my tank, started inside to pay for my gas, walking fast, excited, thinking about those fish, where I should go and ready to get out there.

I snatched open the door to go in, looked up and there's George standing in the doorway, glaring at me, blocking my way.

My hand went in my coat pocket, grasping that ole Smith and Wesson by the handle but keeping it in my pocket, putting my other hand in my other coat pocket, like you do when your hands are cold, only my heart was cold at that moment.

We looked at each other, neither moving.

George sticks out his right hand.

"I'm sorry," he says. "I'm sorry I acted the way I did."

My right hand's on that pistol grip.

I don't know if I want to let go of it. I'm not sure he's sincere and I damn sure don't want 'em to get ahold of me.

Still staring at me out of that Viking, handsome-in-a-goofy-sort-of-way face, he smiles. Still holding out his hand.

I shake it.

"Don't worry about it George," I say and walk past.

I don't believe we talked much again after that, he still came and got a few hamburgers from time to time.

Not long after that Crazy George hitched a ride to one of the local bars with one of his drinking buddies. They proceeded to get good and drunk, drinking til the wee hours of the morning.

I hear that George and his buddy had some kind of disagreement, in their drunken state, and George refused to ride home with his buddy, said he'd walk the ten miles back to Spring Creek, and disappeared in the fog, headed up the highway walking on the centerline.

His buddy, mad, went back in the bar and had another drink. He got ready to go home, jumped in his old station wagon, sped off up the road, went about a mile and ran over George and killed 'em. Didn't even see 'em in the fog, thought he'd hit a deer til he went back and looked.

Totaled his car out too, hitting that rock of a man that George was.

I think George would have been proud of that.

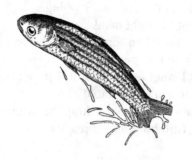

Live Oak Redheads

I wasn't there but I can just see it.

Bruce and Jeff had caught everything just right. The wind, the weather, and the redheads were pouring into their decoys like every duck hunter dreams of.

Didn't matter if you were standing in the middle of the decoys trying to pick up a shot down duck, they'd come in anyway. You couldn't shoot one bunch, reload, and get ready fast enough.

The only problems that day was the limit is two redheads per person, and there wasn't enough seaweed washed up on shore around Bruce and Jeff's blind.

You know how seaweed looks when it's piled up in perfect contour to the high water line, all bunched up about a foot thick, two feet wide, sort of looks like a giant unending sausage going in both directions as far as you can see down the shore.

Bruce and Jeff needed more dead seaweed. They needed it about 2 feet deep and 5 feet wide and because they didn't have enough they had to stop shooting ducks. The reason is, they didn't have anywhere to hide any more birds. They had passed the limit five minutes after they had gotten set up and had kept right on going, not looking back.

Every time they'd shoot and retrieve their birds they'd hide 'em under the piled up seaweed and they had run out of room.

They'd wade out, pick up two or three birds, lift up the seaweed and there'd already be birds under it. For twenty yards around the blind you couldn't stash another bird. They figured if the warden did come up he couldn't help but find their birds, he'd probably trip over one or two.

Time to stop and time to go; in a hurry.

They got lucky that time.

The ducks got lucky too.

Lucky for them there wasn't more seaweed piled around.

Call of the Wild, 1999

What power is it that draws some of us to a life of adventure outdoors?

Is it the danger?

Is it the lure of the unknown?

Is it the excitement and the challenge of pitting yourself against Mother Nature and all of her elements to harvest some of her crops, be they on land, in the sea or in the air?

Farmers and Commercial fishermen are the only modern day challengers. Commercial hunters and trappers have long been pushed to extinction by modern society and so called "progress". Productive wilderness areas have all been tamed by highways, bull doziers, drainage ditches and air conditioning. Florida would still be the wild, raw, game infested, Indian controlled territory that it was a hundred years ago, had it not been for the air conditioner that allows us to retreat indoors from the high humidity and the vicious bugs that protected our state from invasion prior to its invention.

But back to the power, the call of the wild.

Those of us who hear its call, have long ago quit questioning it. We just respond to it. For many, in the not too distant past, the call could be profitable. The gold seekers, the fur trappers, the stone crabbers and lobster fishermen. Even the mullet fisherman could squeeze a good living out of the bay, answering to no one but God.

Time moves on, things and people change, but some of us can't. Some of us feel we just couldn't live if we worked eight to five, closed in a building with rules and structured work loads.

To climb into our slickers suits, load the boat with gas and ice, check our nets and gear and roar off into the rising sun, knowing the unexpected will occur, knowing there's no guarantees or minimum wage. Maybe it's the "not knowing" that keeps us hooked. The lure that dangles daily in front of us. It's the "not knowing" that makes boredom and complacency words not in our vocabulary. Words we can't have in our lives upon penalty of injury or even death if we're not constantly on guard and paying attention.

Thunder storms, lightening, cold fronts, rouge waves, hidden rocks and logs, engine failure, fouled trap lines, slippery decks, sun stroke, razor sharp knives, sharks, freezing weather, fog, skin cancer and the possibility of drowning all wait for the unwary.

Free, wild independence, that must be it. That's what makes us go day in and day out. Being able to whoop and holler at the top of your lungs, when the catch is good, or cry and cuss in a fit of rage when things go bad, without any inhibition cause there's no one around to judge you or wonder if you're crazy.

To be able to totally turn yourself loose, expend all your energy, attempt the impossible, not eat, not sleep, drive yourself to exhaustion in your quest to catch or capture the resource to ensure your existence for another day. That's the call of the wild 1999. That's the call that's still alive in some of us in these modern civilized times. Let's don't stomp this emotion out of all of us, for there are still many things men can't produce in generic form. There are still many products that only Mother Nature can provide and many still-to-be discovered items she hasn't shown us yet.

We need to ensure that those that answer to this silent call are kept alive and well in our society. For in my belief when all these people have been legislated or harassed or stressed out of existence, that will mark the beginning of the end of our civilization as we know it. Mother nature is the ultimate provider for all of our lives and we need those that understand her, can deal with her, and love her.

We will always need those that can answer the call of the wild in 1999 and beyond.

Howling

Have you ever howled?

I mean turned loose, wide open, loud as you can, howled?

You can't do it in public.

You can't do it anywhere anybody can hear.

When I say anybody, I mean anybody that's in hearing distance that doesn't know you.

We do it as a family on rare occasions and everybody loves it, when you finally can talk 'em into it.

It feels great, relaxing, natural when you turn loose.

You got to turn loose.

You can't do it in the normal human posture of speaking. You've got to throw your head back, letting it be a straight line from your lungs, through your throat and windpipe and out your mouth.

Got to close your eyes, which seems natural when your heads thrown back.

You can vary the pitch and cadence by the shape of your mouth and moving your bottom jaw up and down.

It's easy.

Deserted islands like Dog Island are a good place. We've stood on the beach many times, me, Ben, Clay, Mary Jane, howling and barking at the moon. Riverbluff in Georgia is my favorite place.

You get answered.

The coyotes respond. Many times from many different directions. It's great to communicate with something wild, really fires you up and really makes you howl.

My youngest son, Clay, got a demerit at Catholic school for howling in the bathroom while taking a leak.

I didn't get mad.

I understood.

The acoustics were too good in that old fashioned, ceramic tile bathroom to pass up.

I'd of done it myself.

Another kid even joined in, completely innocent, just caught up by the natural instinct of the moment. Bet the duet sounded good. Brought teachers from all over the school. Stopped classes.

I was kinda proud but I told him not to do it again; in school.

Dark nites are good, with the stars all shining bright. The milky way like smoke.

Full moon's good too.

You won't believe the feeling that you get.

The strain in your shoulders melts away.

The worries and the cares of your life go out your throat with the sound.

Every time it's different.

Sometimes you sound lonely.

Sometimes you sound sad.

Sometimes you sound excited and challenging and then sometimes you just sound wild and free and feel that way, specially when something's answering you, inviting you to join 'em. You know they are.

Be careful with it.

Only do it with people you know well, but try it.

Don't get carried away, it's habit forming.

Try it alone for the first time.

If you're fortunate enough to know a proper place.

Let it loose, long notes, aah ooooooooooo til you're almost out of breath then, yip, yip, yip.

You'll be glad you did.

It feels great.

It'll let you know you're still an animal, civilized, cultured, educated, spoiled, but still an animal. Elevated above most all creatures on earth in thought and actions, but still heart, blood, bone, teeth and hair.

There's not much difference between us and them.

Only in our minds.

REDFISH IN THE BASIN   CLAY MARSHALL LOVEL   7-5-99

Redfish In The Basin

Graves Creek is a large, rocky, deep holed creek system on the northeast side of Goose Creek Bay. When the weather turns cold the mullet fill those rocky holes up. The trout and redfish follow the mullet, sometimes gathering up in huge bunches.

There are times when the creek just plain won't hold 'em all and the redfish have to settle in a little basin, about 10 acres, out from the mouth of Graves Creek.

This particular morning that I'm talking about was cold, clear and calm. The north wind had blown hard all-night and combined with the full moon had dried up Goose Creek Bay, making it hard to get around in my old mullet skiff. The wind had laid at daylight, the water was crystal clear and we were searching to find where the mullet had holed up.

I had that old 40 horse wound up as tight as it would go, trying to keep from going aground so I could make it to that little basin as mentioned before. That basin always held about 18" to 2 feet of water on the lowest tides, and usually held a few fish.

When I got about 100 yards from the basin I noticed that calm, slick water in the basin begin to shake and vibrate. As I finally jumped my boat over into that basin the whole basin rose up and exploded into motion.

Every redfish in the Gulf of Mexico must have settled in there, on that low tide.

The water was so full of redfish that they were about to tear the motor handle from my hand as I tried to run the boat, slamming into the foot of the motor and running into the prop. The clear water of the basin instantly turned to chocolate milk from the thousands of redfish boiling up the mud in their panic. Behind the boat in our mud wake were dozens of redfish bobbin' around, swimming on their sides with their head outta the water, dead and dying from getting hit by the prop. There was a two-foot wave of water like a small tidal wave moving over the flats as some of the redfish piled on top of each other, made their escape from that basin over the shallow flats.

I shut the motor off, not wanting to kill or injure any more fish than I already had and they still continued to hit the sides and bottom of the boat and beat against the foot of the motor. You could see dozens of whole redfish completely exposed and out of the water squirming and thrashing around trying to get down in the water but couldn't, because redfish were packed underneath 'em from the surface to the bottom. There were just too many fish for the amount of water they were in and couldn't fit back in the water in their panic.

There is no market for redfish. The State of Florida took 'em away from commercial fisherman and made them a sports fish. We can possess only one, which we picked up out of the water, a casualty from the 40 horse. The eagles, ospreys and crabs enjoyed the rest of the redfish that we had accidentally killed, nothing goes to waste in the sea.

The fish settled down after we cut the motor off, some of them sliding out across the flats, most of 'em just laying quiet, waiting on the tide.

We pulled the boat up towards Grave Creek, found us a little drain deep enough to put the motor down, fired her up and went back to looking for mullet.

Acquiring the ACE

I looked for an offshore boat for two or three years.

I wanted something to grouper fish, set nets offshore and stone crab with.

When my grandfather died down in South Florida I stumbled across the ACE, a 32 foot, custom built, mahogany work boat. Bought it from Mr. A.C. Emmerton, that's where the name ACE comes from.

Mr. Emmerton had cancer too.

That's what my grandfather, Mr. Walt Walton had died from and that's why I was down there.

Mr. Emmerton was dying and he knew it. Selling the ACE was something he really didn't want to do.

Selling the ACE was a final act in admitting that all the things you dreamed of doing weren't going to get done. That you had all the fun you were going to have on this earth, that there weren't going to be anymore offshore adventures that you loved so.

Mr. Emmerton and I hit it off like we'd known each other forever. We watched the evening news, discussed fishing in different parts of the state and just sorta got acquainted.

I loved the ACE and knew I was going to buy it, but I felt that I had to haggle a little bit just to be sociable.

Mr. Emmerton haggled back a little bit too.

I could tell he wanted me to have it.

I wanted it.

I agreed to his price.

We shook hands and I thanked him and wrote him a deposit check, started asking all kinds of questions about the gear on the boat, the services it might need and so on.

Mr. Emmerton seemed to have his mind on something else.

He asked if I would excuse him for just a minute and he walked out the side door of the house into the carport.

I sat down and chatted with Mrs. Emmerton for a minute or two and then heard something from out in the carport, just a noise of some kind, thought it might be Mr. Emmerton moving something around and needed some help.

So I walked out in the carport.

And there sat Mr. Emmerton.

And he was crying. Not making any noise, but sort of sobbing with his head in his hands and his elbow on his knees. Sitting on a short stool with his thin, bony shoulders bobbin up and down through his white T-shirt.

Surrounded by all his fishing gear for the ACE.

Grouper rods, mackerel rods, anchors, electric motors for automatic reels, gaffs, buckets, lures, hooks, leader wire, rope, ice boxes, knives, spot lights, rifles, motor oil, bottom machines, a loran, Everything and anything you'd need to make a trip.

But nothing he needed anymore.

Not for the trip he was going on.

Mr. Emmerton was saying goodbye in his carport that night.

All I could do was pat him on the back and cry a little too.

There wasn't anything to say.

A.C. EMMERTON GOES ON   CLAY MARSHALL LOVEL   6-17-99

A.C. Emmerton Goes On

I bought a boat, the ACE, from Mr. A.C. Emmerton who had terminal cancer and knew he was going to die.

The boat came fully rigged, with an auto pilot, loran, compass, tools, leader, hooks, leads, spare clean clothes, the works. It was his pride and joy and he hated to give it up.

It's a great boat, New England style lobster boat hull, 32 feet long, 11 feet wide, take more sea than you want to be on it in.

We had the boat about 6 months and were fishing it hard for Amberjacks 30 to 40 miles offshore.

The weather had kicked up bad for 3 days and we had the ACE loaded with ice, groceries, bait and fuel waiting for a break in the weather to go out.

It was in March and we had been stuck at the dock and fish house since daylight while it blew and rained. We listened to the weather band on the VHF, chomping at the bit for any sign of a break so we could get at those A.J.'s.

About noon to 1 o'clock the wind slacked, the rain quit and we took our chances and left for the "Dragline", our nickname for our favorite amberjack spot.

The seas were still running about 6 to 7 feet and lead gray like the sky, but the ACE could handle that no sweat.

We reached the "Dragline" about six that evening, anchored down and caught three big A.J.s in the 60-80 pound class before it got full dark and they quit biting.

We got out our little battery operated t.v. and the frying pan and started trying to cook supper and watch the weather.

We couldn't do either one.

The frying pan wouldn't stay on the stove and the t.v. wouldn't stay on the dash unless you held it with both hands.

It had gotten rougher at dark instead of calmer and we decided we would try to make Dog Island 35 miles away before it got really bad.

It was slow go, running with a following sea that was shoving the bow down clear to the windshield in the wall of water called a wave that ran ahead of us.

You couldn't see anything but black water and white wave crests til the lightning started. It struck with foot wide bolts all around us every thirty seconds and fried our loran, our main navigational device.

The rain came in sheets, then the hail started.

The waves got bigger and bigger picking the back end of the ACE up

95

doubling its speed for two seconds to drive it into the back of the 10 and 12 foot walls of water ahead.

The two deck hands put on two life jackets apiece.

The autopilot shorted out.

No loran.

Good ole dependable compass.

Thank God they're fool proof and non electronic.

Water's pouring through the front hatch cover from the bow being shoved down so far. Spray's flying over the side and running through the scuppers.

Rain, hail, rough seas, constant lightning.

Big white eyeballs on everybody when the lightning flashed.

Then the compass, the good ole trusty compass, Mr. Emmerton's compass, spun around 180 degrees and locked up.

Never to move again.

Beat on it, tap on it, cuss it. Stuck.

"What in the hell's going on?"

Is this a nightmare?

Have we offended somebody or something?

Why is so much happening wrong at the same time?

The lightning stops.

The rains stops.

The wind settles some and the seas along with it.

We spot a tower with red-blinking lights on the black horizon that we know to be Carrabelle. We can guide on that to the island.

We slide into the dock at about one A.M.

Happy, happy, happy.

You'd think it was 7 o'clock and we were going to a party.

We had one.

Steaks, fried potatoes, salad, sausage hor'douves, whiskey, beer and wine and then a few hours sleep.

Beautiful the next day.

We go back offshore and have a mediocre fishing trip after picking up a new compass in Carrabelle.

Never could get the old one to move, even after we took it out of the dash. I shook it a few times and then tossed it overboard.

Wish I'd have taken notice of which direction that old compass was pointing when it locked but I didn't. That would have been an interesting thing to know and speculate on later.

The night we got back I got a phone call at the restaurant from Mrs. Emmerton.

She called to tell me that Ace, that's what she called Mr. Emmerton, had died the night before. The night we were in that freaky storm, the night everything went haywire on the boat.

She told me that Ace had asked her to leave the room early that night at 10 o'clock, about the time the storm really got going. She said she didn't mean to but she fell asleep for two hours, cause Ace had seemed real agitated and she wanted to check on him.

She got up at twelve and he was dead.

Died between ten and twelve o'clock.

Died exactly during that time that we were wondering what was going on with the weather and the equipment.

Died during that time when we were thinking that we might be going on that same trip he was going on.

Maybe all that was going on around us was just Ace leaving and gathering up all his spirit for the trip.

I just wish I'd paid attention to what direction that compass was pointing on its last spin of the dial, I'll bet it was pointing toward Ace.

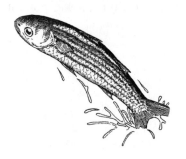

George Falls In

The ACE was a good boat.

It was 32 feet long, 11 feet wide, made of mahogany with a deep keel and a 6 cylinder Perkins diesel. A real work boat and that's what we did with it. Everything from stone crab to grouper fish, to set-net for pompano on Dog Island.

We had some good times and some rough times on that old boat.

This tale's about one of the silly times.

Billy and George used to offshore fish for me on the ACE. They were great fisherman and could bring the grouper home if anybody could. The only problem being, is that they tended to drink on the way in, and sometimes could be in pretty good shape (or bad) when they got to the dock.

This particular time they went in to Shell Point Marina to fuel up for their next trip.

George, Billy's right hand man and deck hand, had him a few Lord Calverts during the slow ride home and was on the ACE, tying it to the fuel dock, when somehow he fell overboard.

Billy, hearing the splash and commotion, comes outta the cabin to see what's going on.

There's George, gasping and splashing and paddling, trying to stay on the surface and breathe. George being the good commercial offshore fisherman that he is, has never learned to swim and Billy knows it.

Billy, not really wanting to get wet, tries to reach George from the boat but he can't.

George goes under for the first time.

He fights his way back to the top to gasp and yell for help.

Billy tries to reach 'em again but fails.

George goes under for the second time.

But he fights his way back up flailing and thrashing cause he knows he going to drown.

Billy can't reach 'em. Billy also knows the water's cold.

George goes down for the third, and usually famous for, final time.

As bad as he doesn't want to, Billy knows he's got to dive in after George and save 'em, so he jumps in, grabs George and stands up! The water's only 3 feet deep!

"George!" Billy says.

"You could have stood up!" "The bottom's right here!"

George replies, gasping and choking for air, "Billy, I wasn't looking for the bottom".

And we think we're good?

Cold, rainy, gray, soggy, nasty, windy.

That's how it was when I left the dock in my old mullet skiff to check out Walker Creek.

The days and days of winter rain draining through the swamps had dyed the water of the bay a dark tea color, making it hard to see if there were any fish in the deep holes.

The tide was low so I ran up Walker Creek as far as I could go, looking for any signs of fish.

There were signs of fish everywhere I looked, but the current was running hard toward low tide and I couldn't get up the shallow drains to where the fish were in my boat.

I decided the best thing to do was to wait on the tide to slack and then to "blind strike" the deep holes between the oyster bars. Low tide was an hour or so away. It was cold, wet and uncomfortable so I ran the mile or so to my buddy Johnny's house to get some coffee and see if he wanted to help me catch some fish.

That day I had it figured right. Most days you don't, but that day I did.

The tide slacked, though the wind and rain had not. We went back up Walker Creek. As we approached the first deep hole just south of Redfish Creek, I motioned for Johnny to pitch out the staff on the edge of the bar.

At that time I was fishing about 500 yards of inch and three quarters monofilament net and I proceeded to pen the entire deep hole around the edges and then put the rest of the net inside the circle like a cinnamon roll; round, round and round, getting smaller with each circle til there's nowhere else to go.

We didn't see a fish til I started about the third lap inside the circle. They'd all been laying quiet in the bottom of the hole cause all the water had drained out of all the little side creeks and washes.

But when they (the fish) made their move, they put on a show. Fish jumping the net, fish jumping in the boat, hitting the side of the boat. Foam was flying all around the cork line, tails sticking up everywhere as those big beautiful run mullet gilled off.

Johnny and I tend to get excited when we hit a good lick. I guarantee that Crazy Horse, Sitting Bull and all the Indians of the world would be proud of the war cries, hooting and hollering that we put out on a good strike.

Johnny and I tend to get really cocky and brag on what good fishermen we are as we take up the net and shuck mullet into the box. We also get real generous with our fish when we catch a lot, throwing mullet to different critters that come around while we're taking up the net.

That year we had some eagles that always hung close by. The birds lived up Walker Creek and around Sheppard Springs and tended to watch us and circle overhead cause we would always feed 'em a mullet.

That particular day there was one lone eagle, sitting on a limb of an old dead knarled cedar tree that grew out of an old Indian shell mound a hundred yards or so from where we had struck the fish. The tide was real low with the oyster bars sticking up three feet or so outta the water. We were chuckling and bragging on ourselves and what good fishermen we were to be able to catch fish like only we could, when we spied that eagle waiting to be fed.

J.R. side-armed a big two-pound mullet toward the bird and the bird knew what was going on the minute the fish went in the air.

But Johnny had thrown that mullet too hard, and it landed high and dry up on that oyster bar with all those sharp shells sticking up.

That eagle must have been listening to us brag and brag.

He must have decided to show us what a real fisherman is and how he can catch fish under hard conditions too.

That bird climbed up and got him some diving room and down he came, wide-open in a dive straight for that dry, sharp oyster bar with the mullet on it.

Johnny and I looked at each other and wondered out loud what the hell that bird was doing besides killing hisself.

At the last split second, before crashing in a full blown dive on that bar, that eagle turned sideways, flicked out one great yellow and black claw and picked that flopping fish up and flew back to his cedar tree.

We cheered that bird like he'd won a gold medal at the Olympics, beating each other's backs and rebel yelling.

And we thought we were good?

EAGLE   CLAY MARSHALL LOVEL   10-8-99

More About Eagles

All the time we spent in the bay around this beautiful wild area we work in, has given us the opportunity to observe nature and her creatures to an extent that most people don't get.

Bald eagles are an everyday site, but one you don't seem to get tired of, especially some of the antics they do.

One memorable thing that Ben and I witnessed was in February or March when we were netting mullet up in the butts of some of the little rocky creeks that wind their way through the marsh grass. These creeks twist and turn and narrow down to eight to twelve feet wide with little pools forming in some of the bends.

We had an eagle that came and circled around, watching us fish, knowing that we would either throw him one or he would find one that had fallen outta the net.

That particular day the creek we were in was narrow and curvy with an open area that was round, and about twenty feet across. That pool was right off the bow of our boat.

The bird would circle and chirp more like a cardinal than an eagle, wanting some food.

I went to throw 'em a mullet, trying to toss the fish across to the other side of the pool. Eagles normally don't like to come within fifty or sixty yards of the boat, but this fish slips in my hand and only falls ten or fifteen feet from us.

When he dove I knew we had never been that close to an eagle before.

When that bird dove from the sky in the classic eagle diving position, the noise from his wings was incredible. It sounded just like the F-16's do before you hear the roar of their engines.

The bird hit the water, I mean hit it hard, reached down deep with his legs and caught that mullet that had sunk. He got up and outta the water like a duck, and flew off.

I never knew they made so much noise with their wings.

I've seen eagles dive bomb buzzards to steal an old dead possum.

I've seen 'em steal butterfish from the ospreys, making 'em drop their catch and then the eagle catching it in mid-air.

I've seen 'em fly off with half-grown live coons in their claws.

I've seen 'em make ospreys drop their fish and then not bother to even retrieve the stolen catch. He was just proving a point. Don't fish in my territory.

My favorite eagle story has a redwing blackbird as the attacker of a full-grown eagle.

As I came in the creek from crabbing, I noticed an eagle soaring above the creek, just drifting on the air currents, flapping his wings just enough to stay afloat. Over his back and occasionally sitting on the eagle's shoulders, was a redwing blackbird, pecking that eagle on the neck and head, squawking and raising cane in general.

The eagle seemed totally unconcerned, drifting around in the air, looking down at the creek, totally intent on other things besides that pesky blackbird.

Without warning the eagle falls in to his classic, catching dive, head down, wings tucked, heading like a shot toward the water. Leaving the blackbird still pecking where the eagle used to be.

At the last second, when it seemed like there's no way for the bird to miss crashing into the water, his big wide yellow claws come up forward of his body, slashing into the surface of the water and up the bird goes with a three foot cottonmouth moccasin writhing and squirming in his claws.

The bird gains altitude and starts flying home. Snake justa twisting and twirling.

The blackbird gets back on the eagle's shoulders and starts pecking his head, and all three of 'em fly away.

The snake not much liking the trip.

Grouper

It's a good sound to wake-up to, that heavy "thump" on the deck. Then the staccato, short drumming that you know is a big grouper slamming his tail up and down, making ya jump outta the bunk and run to your bandit.

Billy's bent over his heavy grouper rod, smiling, saying he thinks he's got two fish on, and he's throwing that damn rod down and switching to his bandit as soon as he can wrestle these two up.

George is on the stern corner of the ACE, jerking on the two hundred pound test mono that's hanging down from his bandit rod, setting the hook on another fish.

My bait's reaching the bottom, line filtering down thru my fingers, and something snatches it hard, before I can tighten the brake on the bandit's reel. As the brake stops the reel from turning, the three-inch pulley, shackled to the end of the rod, starts rattling, then comes tight as the three-foot Kevlar bandit rod bends with the weight of the fish.

The pulley rattles again as another fish hits the second hook, rigged two feet above the bottom one.

I'm reeling now hard and fast as I can go.

I hear another thump and drumming noise, then another as Billy unhooks his two fish, sliding 'em to the stern like beer sliding down a bar, to pile up with the big red grouper George caught earlier. George is swinging two more fish over the side, a red and a black. I'm leaning over the side, having to grab my leader with both hands to lift the weight of two black grouper, ten to twelve pounds a piece, over the rail.

We're in a rally.

We're in exactly what we want to be in, a rally. When the grouper are stacked like cordwood on the bottom, hungry, starving, competing for our baits, cause there's so many more fish than there are hooks with cigar minnows.

Time is of the essence.

The rally can stop as fast as it starts, and we're gonna make hay while the sun shines.

Before my fish makes his slide, to join the other fish at the stern, I'm threading cigar minnows on each hook, dropping the sixteen ounces of lead over the side and paying out line on the bandit reel to make it hit the bottom faster.

Billy's hollering for the gaff, says he's got a twenty, twenty-five pounder to the surface.

We don't want the hook to pull out. That a sixty to eighty dollar fish.

We'll gaff that one and any more like 'em.

Everybody's motion now.

Reel, reel, reel.

Swing 'em over the side.

Twist those circle hooks out.

Grab two baits.

Thread 'em on and throw it overboard, spinning that bandit reel as fast as you can.

Tighten the brake.

Set the hook.

Reel, reel, reel again.

It gets to be work. Hot work in July and August. Messy work. Painful work as your fingers slip into those armored gill plates or toothy mouths. The blood from your fingers mingles with the grouper blood and slime on the deck. You don't feel it, don't care. Mind set on one thing, catching more.

Your bait gets down and there's not an instant bite.

Billy's having to re-rig his line.

George is reeling one up.

I take this short break to throw some of the fish, that George's wading around in at the stern, into the ice box. I get about three of 'em picked up and I hear my bandit rattle, and see the rod point toward the bottom.

"Fish on," Billy yells, pulling knots tight with his teeth.

I scramble to my bandit, not having to set the hook, just reeling away.

You can put some kinda fish on the boat in a hurry with a bandit. It being bolted to the boat, loaded with heavy line, the reel you crank like an ice cream churn, taking up two feet with every turn. No drag. No give. No play. A meat machine. They either come on up or the hook tears out. No messing around with 'em. Put 'em on the boat.

They're a pretty sight, those grouper are, red ones and black. Gills all flared out, jaws popping, white mouth big enough to put a cantaloupe in. Fins standing straight up, eyes bulged.

Black grouper are long and sleek like a big fresh water bass with teeth, black and gray splotted with white on their sides and bellies.

Red grouper are chunky and thick like a lineman on the football team. Shorter and stouter than their cousins, bigger heads. They eat like hogs, anything they can get, including their own kind when you run outta bait.

They're slowing down now. The bites are less aggressive, more time between 'em, giving us a few minutes to try to get all these fish in the box. The pile of red and black bodies, flopping and gasping, sliding back and forth with the roll of the boat. Stacking up around George's feet when the boat rolls his way, sliding away to pile up in the other corner when the boat rolls back with the swells.

We're still picking one off here and there, but quite a few minutes now between bites. The tides changed, either swinging us off the spot or changing the fish's appetite.

We're pleased and happy with the forty or fifty fish we've hauled up.

Four to five hundred pounds of good eating, a delicacy, caught in thirty minutes.

We love it, joking and teasing, still fishing but working on other things. Re-rigging lines, icing the catch, thawing more bait, washing the deck, still responding to the occasional bite.

Then they stop completely.

No bites.

No fish showing on the recorder.

Time to move.

On to the next bite knowing that rallies are few and far between, but always hoping. Every rock you stop on an anticipation of another rally.

One grouper here.

Three on the next spot.

None on this one.

None on that one.

None on another one.

Anchor down twenty or thirty times a day, til black dark, looking for another payday.

Two, sometimes three days of hunting, an easy hundred different stops. A hundred different times of anchoring down and pulling the anchor up. The rally the lure that keeps us going.

If we're lucky we'll have one or two rallys a trip, making it a real good trip. Twelve or fifteen hundred pounds of grouper, a cobia or two, a few snapper, some amberjack. A decent payday for us. Not that way all the time. Sometimes we're lucky to make expenses.

A curious thing happened once and I've got witnesses to it.

I was gutting a black grouper we'd caught in eighty feet of water, off Dog Island. I stuck the knife in his belly and split 'em up to his throat. When I drew the knife out there were feathers stuck to the blade. Knowing something unusual was going on, I got Joby, who was patching his cast net, to come watch as I removed the belly-sack from this ten pound black grouper. Cutting the end off the belly-sack and mashing it, out slides a whole bird that grouper had managed to catch. Knowing that you can't make a bird sink, even when it's dead, that told me that grouper might sometimes feed right on the surface.

I just thought it strange that a creature of the air, (I think it was a purple martin), that lives at the highest parts of our world, could wind up in the belly of a creature that lives in the lowest part of our world, at the bottom of the sea.

Grouper fishing is great when you're catching 'em, a terrible chore when you're not, but grouper themselves are great all the time.

Runnin' Home

Three days out, was about all we seemed to could stand. Three days of grouper fishing from daylight to black dark, confined to the deck space of the Ace, not having a good shower or bath, smelling like fish and staying damp was all the fun we wanted.

Billy captained my boat. I deck handed for 'em and he always fished til the stars came out 'fore he headed home. He'd punch in the Shell Point Beacon on the loran and take-off wide open at the break-neck speed of ten knots. Spring Creek always seemed to be fifty-sixty miles away, so it's easy to figure the trip home was at least five hours. It'd be nine when we started, so that would make it at least 2 or 3 a.m. when we hit the hill.

Here's the normal routine for the long ride.

Billy's in the driver's seat, feet propped on the dash, autopilot on, Lord Calvert in his hand.

Me and George on the back deck, ice boxes open, gutting and packing fish.

If we'd had a good day that might take a half-hour or so, another thirty minutes to stow the gear and scrub the boat.

Then we'd mix a drink.

Me rum and orange juice with half a lime.

George a Lord Calvert, freshening Billy's drink while he's making his.

Seemed like everybody sorta drifted to their own private parts of the boat for a while. Sipping their drink, staring at the night sky. The rumble of the diesel, the rush of the water going by, the boat lulling us all into a peaceful trance for a spell.

Then somebody'd get hungry.

I'd go into the cab, fire off the alcohol stove, while George dug around the iceboxes looking for something to cook. Most times we'd eaten everything we had so we'd skin a grouper out, or a scamp if we had it, and fry 'em up.

Always had onion.

Good ole onions. Skin 'em, cut 'em in quarters, drop 'em in the hot grease. Instant mouth watering smells fill the boat.

Cook those grouper fingers golden brown, burn those onions almost black and sprinkle 'em with salt and dig in.

Billy's still driving, drink in one hand, grouper and onions in the other.

George is eating too and fixing drinks.

I'm eating and drinking, cleaning up the stove 'fore that squall hits that's flashing in the distance. It's slick calm now but the lightning and the

111

fresh coolness of the air tells us we're gonna get a little wind and rain.

Billy's got a full belly now. He's had two or three Lord Calverts and he always does the same thing.

He tells me he wants to lay down for just a few minutes and if I'll run the boat, he'll relieve me in a little while.

I laugh, gathering up everything I need close at hand for the long run home, cause I know Billy's fixing to crawl in the bunk, go hard snoring asleep and not wake up til I yell at 'em to help me tie the boat to the dock.

George won't be long behind Billy crawling in the other bunk.

I'll have the boat, the Gulf, the sky and the weather to myself and to tell you the truth, I kinda liked it that way. Glancing at the loran, checking the compass, watching through the black windshield.

Lot of times, if it wasn't real rough or raining too hard, I'd hang my head out the side window, like a train engineer and ride for miles feeling the wind, looking at the stars, listening to our wake peeling out from under the bow. Running a thousand thoughts through my mind, trying to discard any that don't feel good.

The rain starts, I have to duck back inside, sliding the window shut. The bow starts to rise and fall a little bit and a light spray's crossing the stern. The only light is the greenish-yellow light of the loran numbers that are guiding us home, counting down the miles, pointing the direction.

Number twenty-four buoy's coming up soon. We want to stay on the right side of that, and off the reef.

Can't see anything with the rain, the boats like a little capsule, suspended in black water, from above and below, then a lightning flash shows lots of white on the wave tops. Shows twenty-four buoy where it's supposed to be, that loran's the ticket.

Hour or so to go, then the fun part.

Picking your way through Spring Creek's many dog legged channels, in the dark, with the tide falling.

There's Shell Point, twinkling in the distance, then Oyster Bay when the boat's on top of a wave.

One little light, like a too-low star, glowing in the black tree line tells me Spring Creek's still there.

The rain stopped, low moon in the west sky. My head's out the side window again and we're roaring back and forth, right then left down that dog-leg channel at the full ten knots. No spotlight needed, the channel markers like thin, black, round, soldiers at attention in the now slick water.

It almost seems sinful to back down that Perkins diesel to idle from its 2200 RPM's, that's been singing to, and vibrating us for five or six hours. That's kept Billy and George hard asleep, like babies in a car, all the way in. They're up now though, on their own, the change in sound waking 'em up. Yawning, stretching, peeing over the side, Billy saying the same ole thing, he can't believe he slept that long.

George hops on the dock and ties us up, as I back her in.

When I shut the engine down the silence is heavy. Words sound strange in a normal voice, not having to shout over the diesel.

Spring Creek's quiet at three a.m. You can hear dew dripping off the oak leaves as you get in the truck. A shower's on your mind now and a soft, clean bed with the air conditioner down low.

Clean, dry and cool.

That's all I want right now.

Food can come tomorrow.

After some sleep.

It Changed His Life

Billy is one of my best friends. I'm lucky enough to have three or four and Billy is definitely one of those.

We've done a lot together. Bitched and moaned about business, laughed, fished, drank and dreamed, but I did Billy a terrible service once.

I carried 'em mullet fishing when the fish were running.

I'd had to call Billy at midnight to come help me pack fish. Bobby, Don, Jake, Ben and me, we'd all caught a load and needed help icing and stacking 'em. Billy came right on down, jumped in and helped and we finished up about 2:30 a.m.

I told Billy I was gonna lay down for a few hours and go back out, about daylight.

I got up about 6:30, walked down to the fish house and found Billy curled up on a bench, sound asleep. I woke 'em up, gave him some coffee and started putting on my slicker to go fishing.

I asked Billy if he wanted to go with me, handing 'em an extra slicker suit and pointing out some boots.

He made the mistake of accepting my offer, putting on that slicker and crawling in the boat.

I was fixing to change his life and didn't know it.

We still argue about whether it was good or bad.

It's cloudy, early December, not much wind, kinda cold. We clear the canal, I twist the handle on that forty-horse, pointing the boat east. We run about a mile, I look up and see mullet jumping, thirty or forty at a time, on a sand flat off Cedar Creek. We hadn't been gone from the dock three minutes.

Without slowing down, I run to the head of the school of mullet, pitch out the staff on the end of my net and take 'em in.

The fish go in the air by the hundreds when I get the circle closed. Billy's whooping and hollering like a madman. As I jump the boat over inside the circle and start winding 'em down with the rest of my net, the fish are in a solid wall, jumping the corkline, hitting the side of the boat, a dozen two-pound fish jump in the boat. I look back and Billy's standing on the now empty net table. He's got big, red roe mullet in each hand, holding 'em over his head like a referee signaling "touchdown", dancing like an Indian, yelling, "I like this, I like this, I really like this."

We start clearing the net, shucking seven, eight hundred pounds of run mullet, filling the ice box and having to put fish in the bottom of the boat.

We get cleared up, run around the end of Shell Point and strike again.

That lick and one more gives us all the boat'll float. We go in and unload.

Billy's excited and he's thinking out loud.

"Daddy's got an old tunnel boat under the house that hadn't been used in years."

"I think that old thirty horse on the bream boat'll push it."

"I wonder if Daddy's old nets are any good anymore?"

"What kinda nets do I need to catch these run fish?" and on and on.

I'll say this for 'em, he was determined.

Two days later, me and J.R. are sitting at the Shell Point run stand, waiting on fish to drop out, when we look up and see a boat coming.

"Who's that?"

"I don't know, ain't seen a boat like that before."

This multi-colored mullet boat's pulling up with a pile of net on the back, and it's Billy, with George, his grouper fishing deckhand, holding the staff and shaking his head, very skeptical like.

Billy and George gave the mullet a fit that year. Billy being one of those people that's a natural fisherman and hunter. They made a few mistakes, like we all do, but we gave 'em a few pointers and they had some good catches.

The mullet bug had bit Billy hard.

He had a bad case of it and he chased 'em day and night during run season, til the net ban.

We understood. We'd all been bit years ago.

It changed my life, twenty-two years ago when I first penned a bunch of fish.

I still hadn't gotten over it and hope I never do.

SHARKS   CLAY MARSHALL LOVEL   7-18-99

118

Sharks

I've always been interested in sharks. Scared of 'em, fascinated with 'em. I've been around a lot of 'em commercial fishing like we do. Gotten to catch 'em, kill 'em, touch 'em, sell 'em, cut 'em, cuss 'em but most of all, respect 'em. Here's a few of my encounters, plus one or two that were told to me, first hand accounts.

The first shark and the only shark I've ever encountered when I was swimming was when I was about ten years old. My Grandfather, Walt Walton and I were living on his boat and cruising the Bahamas.

Every afternoon we'd anchor down off of some little island and dive up dinner. Mostly lobster and a few small fish I could get with a little three-foot spear.

I was snorkeling around, sticking a few lobster, looking under coral heads in about five feet of water, thirty yards from the boat. I'm looking at all the pretty little tropical fish, the coral, the sponges when all of a sudden I look in a bright clear sandy place between the rocks and there's a shark.

My gut tightens up. My heart starts to race making my ears beat like a drum. I can't take my eyes off 'em and I need to go to the top to get a breath.

What'll I do.

I'm floating on the top now, trying to breath regular through my snorkel. I'm sure I probably sounded like a whale with all the air and water I was moving through that tube, excited as I was.

I've got my spear pointed toward this man-eating monster that's all of two and a half, to three feet long, acting like it's asleep lying there in that patch of sunlight on the bottom.

I know as soon as I turn my back on 'em he'll come up behind me and take a big bite, probably one leg or an arm. I can't take my eyes off of 'em for a minute.

I know what I'll do.

I'll attack.

While he's pretending to be asleep I'll dive down on 'em, and with all my strength drive this spear in his head.

Before I can think about it too much I suck in a deep breath, dive the five feet to the bottom and stick this sleeping monster. (I know now that it was a two-foot nurse shark taking a nap).

The gig comes alive in my hands, twisting and turning. The whole world turns to silt and sand, I can't see the shark wiggling on the end of my gig and that really scares me. I know he's going to bust outta that cloud of silt and bite my foot off.

Panic and fear take over, mostly imagination. I give an underwater scream, let go of the gig and strike out for the boat, swimming for my life.

I guess that two-foot shark couldn't catch me, dragging along that gig sticking out of 'em. Seemed like a close call at ten years old.

I've caught and seen a lot of sharks since then.

Mark and I hooked and fought a twelve-foot hammerhead off the west end of Dog Island. I put a whole clip of .30 caliber bullets in 'em and still didn't whip 'em. He drug us for miles up and down the bay in my little sixteen-foot skiff.

I've fought an eighty-pound tarpon for an hour at midnight off the beach at Dog Island. I had 'em whipped on a nine-foot surf rod and Bobby was out in the water about knee deep, grabbing my leader to slide the big silver fish up on the beach when all hell broke loose right at our feet. The tarpon went crazy again, thrashing, jumping, fighting like he was just hooked. The water boiling all around; beaten to foam by a big black trail that appeared like a silent ghost, attached to some monster that's come right up to the dry beach to steal my prize.

Bobby's hollering and yelling, I am too. Water's flying everywhere. Bobby's jumping out of the water like it's scalding hot. I'm trying to keep my fish on my line.

Then quiet.

No more splashing or thrashing, the water settles down to its calm, friendly, smoothness, like it is on pretty nights.

There's still weight on my line but no more fight or pull.

I reel the line in as far as I can to get the leader close to the beach. Nobody wants to wade out to get the leader right now.

My fish is still there, I can see the big silver head and sides of the tarpon in the starlight.

Bobby slides 'em up on the beach and we get a small flashlight and take a look.

One bite's been taken from the underside of the tarpon. It looks like you used a cookie cutter, a big cookie cutter. The bite's clean, except for a few little ragged pieces of meat hanging down. Every tooth mark shows up where the shark bit through, back bone and all, like a half-moon shape missing from the belly of my fish.

The power of those jaws to take a ten or twelve pound bite, eighteen inches across.

I've herded big sharks like cows when I could catch 'em sunning on the reef in two or three feet of water. Staying between them and deep water you can drive 'em where you want.

Sometimes.

Sometimes they do the unexpected and one almost had the last laugh on me one day.

I was standing on the bow of my old mullet skiff, riding the shallows on the Shell Point Reef, when I spied a big Bull shark enjoying the sunshine. He was eight or nine feet long, fat like a catfish, dark gray, just easing along.

He broke for deep water at the approach of my boat and I cut 'em off and drove 'em back to the shallows. He took off down the reef, throwing sand and water with his tail and I fell in right behind 'em, enjoying the chase and just looking at that big critter.

He's about eight feet in front of me, hauling buggy. I'm standing on the bow, twisting the throttle on my motor, watching the shark, trying to anticipate his next move, when the shark does a hundred and eighty degree turn, doubling back underneath the boat. The water's so shallow that there's not room enough for the shark and the foot of my motor. They meet, my motor foot and that shark, and they're both going wide open in opposite directions.

We have one hell of a crash, me perched on that little bow cap like a bird.

The boat's lifted up about two feet, the motor's knocked up clear out of the water to lock into the tilt position, wide open and in gear. I go flying through the air, luckily in the same direction the boat's turning to, and am able to catch the side with one arm, my body hits the water.

Ever see one of those old cowboy movies where the cowboy mounts his horse with his horse running by at full speed? He grabs the horn on the saddle, bounces along beside the horse to gain momentum and then flings himself up into the saddle.

That's how I remounted the boat.

I was sticking like glue to that boat.

You weren't getting me in that water with that critter.

I'm more careful now when I herd up a big one. I stand in the floor of the boat and hold on tight.

We've counted coup on big eight and ten footers, me and the boys, Ben and Clay.

Poked huge sharks, with our oars, just to say we touched 'em. Those big sharks would be in the grass on the shorelines at high tide chasing mullet. Two feet of water, thick with grass for the mullet to hide in and those big sharks would be in the grass with 'em, just hungry I guess.

Let 'Em Go

The closest and most peaceful observation of a really big shark was at Dog Island, on the bay side, right at sunset on a half tide, rising.

Donnie Mock, an old mullet fisherman, had made a strike with his nets earlier in the day just down from the house. He'd caught a few catfish and pinfish with the mullet and had thrown 'em back in the water. The light waves and rising tide had pushed the dead trash fish up to the shore-line.

Mary Jane, Ben, Clay and I were sitting on the porch eating fried mullet and watching the sun go down, when I spied something down the beach. We all went outside to see what it was and boy were we surprised. Right up on the shore, where the catfish and pinfish had washed up, was a big, big shark. He was eating those dead fish like chocolate chip cookies. His head and back were completely out of the water as the water was only a foot deep where his body was, sloping up to dry land where his head and the dead fish were.

I ran back in the house and got my rifle, an old lever action 30-30, yelling at the kids to not get too close til I got there.

We could walk right up to 'em.

We could stand on hard dry land and walk up to a ten-foot shark that was wallowing around and eating like a pig.

What a sight. Massive head, two feet or better wide, dorsal fin sticking up like a small sailboat and back behind this, a big tail sticking up, bent over at the top from its own weight, not designed to be in the air but to be in the water where it would stand up straight, and provide the thrust and power to move that big body.

We stood and watched in awe as that huge creature slid around on the sand in that shallow water looking for more goodies. He moved ten or fifteen yards off the shoreline where the water was about two feet deep, still not deep enough to cover his back, and slowly cruised back and forth searching.

I decided to try an experiment.

I picked up a short stick about two feet long, walked half the distance from the shoreline to the big shark and started swishing the stick in the water, about like you'd beat an egg.

He'd turn right around at the sound and slowly start sliding his way over to me.

I'd get out of the water.

He'd come over to where I used to be, hunt around for a few seconds and then slowly start pushing his way along with that enormous bent-over tail, parallel to the shore.

I walked out toward him again, swished my stick in the water, to make 'em come to me, but this time I had something else in mind.

As the shark started his lazy, slow approach, with his back and the top of his head exposed, I dropped my little stick and put that ole 30-30 to my shoulder, taking a bead on his head.

"Don't shoot 'em," Mary Jane says to me.

I'm taking the slack out of the trigger, focused in on where I'm fixing to send that bullet. He's only about twenty feet away and he's dead if I shoot.

I realize she's right.

In that "Don't shoot 'em" I hear a lot more than just three words. I hear, "hasn't this been a thrill to be so close to something so wild and big." I hear, "look how slow and easy and peaceful and graceful that creature is." I hear, "he's just doing what's natural." I hear, "look what a grand creation of nature he is, in his element on this beautiful evening."

I lower the rifle.

I also get out of the water.

We walk along with 'em as he slides his way past our house. Never hurrying just slow and steady, his whole huge body exposed at times when he crosses little sand bars.

We were fortunate to be able to watch such an animal.

He was fortunate that I have a levelheaded, compassionate, wonderful, beautiful wife.

Personalities

Different species of sharks definitely have distinct, different personalities.

We've caught hundreds if not thousands, of sharks over the years net fishing. Most times the sharks we caught were by catch, set-net fishing for pompano off the beach at Dog Island. We'd keep 'em and sell 'em too. Stumping 'em out, cutting off their heads and tails, saving their fins to dry 'em out and ship 'em up north.

Their different personalities show up when you're clearing 'em from your nets and throwing 'em on the deck.

You've got to picture two men, in a twenty-foot skiff, hauling net over the stern, picking out three to five foot sharks.

Lemon sharks, bonnet heads they thrash around a bit while you're taking 'em outta the net and they flop a little bit on the deck but they're no problem unless you accidentally get your hand in their mouth.

Black tip and white tip sharks are another animal. They're snapping and biting and twisting and turning all the time. You've got to be real careful with them and they don't quit even after they're piled up on the deck of the boat.

As more net comes in and the back of the boat gets heavier, with net and fish, the bow rises up. Those black tip sharks come sliding back to where you're trying to work and it's like a pack of wild bull dogs, snapping and popping their jaws all around your feet. You have to keep kicking 'em back up to the front to keep from getting bit. Heavy rubber boots don't last too long kicking into all those razor sharp teeth.

Black tips live longer after they're taken out of the water than any other sharks I've dealt with.

His Head Itched

Another shark tale we experienced was off Shell Point when Mary Jane, Maureen her sister, Mark and I went trolling for Spanish Mackerel.

It was slick calm about mid-morning on a bright sunny day. We looked up ahead and saw this big dorsal with a tail sticking up behind it and knew it was a good shark.

Mark baited up a big surf caster with a chunk of mullet as I guided the boat as close as we could. Mark casted the bait to the shark and when it hit the water it spooked 'em and he swam away and disappeared.

We left the bait out and since it was pretty and we were hungry, we decide we'd fix some sandwiches and eat right there.

Maureen was sitting on the stern corner of the boat, right next to my old Johnson outboard motor. She's got the bread out and is putting mayo on it for our sandwiches. I'm up in the front of the boat with Mark, and Mary Jane is digging in the ice chest for some drinks.

I happen to look up and here comes that big dorsal fin, slicing the water like a knife, straight for the boat.

I whisper to everybody to be still and quiet as I pick up a big steel harpoon I kept aboard for just this type of event. We want 'em close and we don't want to spook 'em.

Maureen hasn't noticed anything going on, she's intent on slapping mayo on the bread.

I'm just getting ready to make my throw with that harpoon when the shark, about a ten foot hammerhead, slides under the boat, wheels around and starts scratching his big ole hammer-of-a-head on the foot of my motor.

The boat starts to shake a little bit from the scratching. I'm posed like a native with that spear easing to the back of the boat, when Maureen, still holding bread and mayo, looks up at me. I'm going ssshhh, be quiet. She looks to her left and down in the water. About a foot from where she's sitting there's an eye as big as a baseball looking back, attached to the end of that shark's hammer.

This is too much, too quick, for Maureen or most anybody. She screams, throws the bread and the mayo and runs to the front of the boat.

The shark screams too, I guess, cause he hauls ass, never to be seen again.

The Biggest I Saw

The biggest shark I've ever seen; by far, was not offshore on all our deep sea trips but in four feet of water off Long Bar, that's right off the beach at Shell Point.

Bruce and I were fishing mullet hard in those days. We were in Bruce's tunnel boat, a twenty-two footer with eight hundred yards of net. Bruce was standing on the bow cap, I was standing on the ice box. We were both watching a good bunch of fish flipping and a jumping two or three hundred yards down Long Bar. The sun was bright, the water clear. A light breeze was blowing from the west, drifting us from out of the channel on to a bright white sand knot that's on the west end of Long Bar.

As we drifted up on that sand lump, with about four feet of clear water covering it, we were both intent on those mullet. The first clue we had that there was something nearby was when we heard a big "whoosh". The sound of water when something big, really big, stirs it up with its tail.

There's a big boil of water ahead of the boat, sand and shell stirred up in it.

And there he is.

Gliding right beside the boat, not five feet away, effortlessly sliding by from that one thrust of that giant tail is a shark.

We can't believe our eyes.

Bruce got down from the bow, to the deck. I get down from the ice box. Neither one wanting to be perched high, not holding on to anything with this monster going by.

The shark's in no hurry.

We get a long, hard look at an animal that doesn't need to know fear, he's so big.

The boat's twenty-two feet long. The shark's going by slow, exactly parallel to us. He's almost as long as the boat. Conservative, eighteen feet. His dorsal looks to be three feet tall and his girth I can't even guess. A good four-man submarine he'd make hollowed out. Looks like he could swallow a cow with two bites and have room for seconds.

Then he's gone, like he'd never been there. Slid off in the dark channel, swallowed by the deep.

Bruce and I haven't said anything. Just looked at each other and the shark.

"Did you see what I saw?"

"Yeah, I saw it, and it was the damnedest thing I've ever seen."

"Arnold Swartzenegger couldn't throw me outta the boat today."

"I know what you mean."

"I think those mullet have dropped off the bar."

"Let's go get 'em."

The Biggest I Caught

The biggest shark I ever caught, or should say helped catch, was off Key West, twenty or twenty five years ago.

Barney, a retired navy bosun, built like Pop Eye, and Pops, Barney's dad, and I went grouper fishing in my dad's twenty foot Robalo.

No bottom machine, no loran, just a compass. That's all you needed. It was lobster season and all you had to do was find a line of traps set in one spot, and fish. That group of traps was set on a big coral head or pile of rocks and there were always plenty of fish when there was bottom like that.

We'd had a good day catching red and black grouper. I'd caught a Cobia that turned out to weigh sixty-nine pounds. We were about ready to go home the twenty miles or so to Key West, when Barney hooked on to "something good", on his stout, solid glass grouper pole.

As the line peeled off his reel at a moderate but steady pace, I pulled the anchor in and here we went.

Whatever we had on pulled that heavy Robalo, one fifteen Evinrude, three men, ice, fish and beer, steadily through the water. Barney giving 'em hell, putting on the pressure the whole time.

Barney could put considerable pressure on. He was built like a barrel with arms like oak limbs. All his veins were popping out with the strain.

One hour, a steady pulling pace by the fish.

Two hours, it stops and starts again.

Three hours, the fish is barely moving and Barney's giving out.

"He's coming up," Barney yells as he's reeling and gaining line on his reel.

We'd decided it must be a big Jew fish by the way he'd fought, and we wanted 'em.

"Must be a three hundred pounder, maybe more," Barney guesses, sweating and puffing.

I grab the gaff, jump up on the rail of the boat, holding to the tee-top to peer over the side to see what's coming up.

You can see way down in the clear water off the keys. At first I didn't see anything, the fish was still too deep. Then I saw a dark shadow, no form, just mass and movement. Then I saw what it was, coming at a sharp angle up toward the surface.

"It ain't no Jew fish," I yell to Barney and Pops, as I quickly get down off the rail to a more safe and secure place on the deck. "It's the biggest damn shark you've ever seen."

The sharks slowly cruising back and forth underneath the boat, completely tuckered out from fighting Barney and pulling the boat.

We're all speechless looking at 'em over the side. His size is beyond belief to us, and that gaff I'm holding is like a safety pin is to a whale.

This fish is big. We don't know what kind it is, but looking back we think it may have been a white shark. His girth was really impressive, his length, fourteen or fifteen feet, his belly was white, he had a mouth full of teeth that I didn't like looking at. But what I remember most was that big, round, black eye that always seemed to be looking at me.

We got to get 'em home. We were fishing in a tournament and we knew this was the prize money for the biggest fish.

We got to get a rope around 'em, cause I ain't sticking that gaff in something I know weighs a thousand pounds or more.

First, I rig the anchor rope with some weights tied to it to make a big loop and try to get him to swim through it, hoping to lasso 'em that way as he slowly, exhaustedly, glides around the boat.

We're all nervous as hell fiddling with a monster that looks like he could crush the boat if he had the energy.

That black eye seems to be taking me in every time he passes by as I try to get the loop around 'em. But my idea is not working.

Finally, I tell Barney and Pops to get the rope ready. The next time the shark passes by I'm going to gaff the top part of that huge tail, try to roll it up on the rail of the boat so they can tie the rope around it.

I'm as nervous as a mouse stealing cat food but then the shark passes by and I sink that gaff in the tip of his tail and I literally roll over and lay on the deck of the boat, holding to the gaff with all I've got. I can't believe this tail I'm hooked to as Barney and Pops get a rope around it. The top part I've gaffed must be close to three feet long from where it leaves his body. The bottom part not quite as long. The rope is secured to his tail and tied to the stern, the motor's running and I put it in gear and take up slack.

We're gonna drag that monster backwards. I've heard they'll drown unless the water flows forwards through their gills.

It's unreal.

I'm running that one fifteen Evinrude three quarters throttle and we're barely moving. That huge shark on the end of our rope is slowly spinning round and round. Dorsal coming up and over, then the pectoral fins come out and go around, then the dorsal again.

We drag 'em for a good ten minutes, thinking that oughta do 'em.

Now to load 'em up and get 'em home.

We all grab the rope and pull the shark up to the stern, tail first. We bring his tail up in the boat, thinking to tie it off tight to the console and leave the main body of the fish in the water and drag 'em home. We all three pick up the tail and take it forward and look down to find we're standing almost up to our knees in water. Just the weight of that tail and the rear part of his body has got the whole stern sitting under water almost drowning out the motor.

We quickly slide the tail section back out of the boat, the stern comes up.

I'm gonna give you another idea of how big this fish was. It's sort of a gross example, but it has always stuck in my mind.

When we would lift that shark's tail up, trying to secure 'em and haul 'em, his body would be in the water and when we'd all three lift that tail high, the old shark's butt hole would open up and it looked big enough to stick your arm in without touching the sides.

This was a big, heavy shark.

With a bottomless, big black eye, that was always looking at you.

We're trying to get 'em home and can't begin to get 'em in the boat. Don't want 'em in the boat.

We try towing 'em pulled up short to the stern. The bow just rises way up and we barely move.

We try tying 'em up along side head forward. The boat lists so badly that it just wants to go in circles.

We take 'em to the stern again to try and tow 'em back further from the boat than we did earlier. We get all set and I push the throttle wide open on that Evinrude. The motor's screaming, throwing water in a rooster tail behind us. The shark's starting to slide pretty good rolling round and round again like a big finned top. Barney and Pop are sitting as far forward as they can on the bow to try to bring it down so the boat will plane off. We're gaining a little speed, the motor's straining and screaming, when POW, the motor blows, the boat stops and in a rush of water from the momentum he'd gained being towed, that huge, tooth-studded, black eyed shark washes up against the stern.

And he seems to be feeling better.

Thrashing around more.

Breathing faster.

Shaking the boat some every time he wiggles a little bit.

And we're broke down.

Maybe we should let 'em go now while he's still woozy.

Maybe we should let 'em go now before we can't let 'em go or he doesn't want to go since we're sort of, immobile now.

We all agree, as bad as we hate to, to untie the monster.

He sorta half-swims, half sinks outta sight into the gloom below, all of us watching as he disappears.

The last thing I could see as he faded outta sight was the big black eye.

These two stories that follow were told to me by people they happened to.

I believe 'em both.

Charlie's Scare

Charlie, a good customer and the local game warden loved to scuba dive and spearfish. He told me at the restaurant one night, that he'd found some kind of old wreck in forty or fifty feet of water and it was packed full of big grouper. He was looking forward to the next day when he was going back to shoot some.

I saw him a few days later and asked him about the trip and this is what he told me.

When he anchored down that morning the weather was pretty and to look in it, the water was clear. But when he got down to the last eight or ten feet of water close to the bottom, there was an algae bloom or something that made the water murky, dark and hard to see in. But Charlie being the hunter that he is, didn't let this stop 'em. He just fired up an underwater light, shone the grouper in the wreck and shot 'em.

He said he had a big red grouper on the string on his spear gun, the grouper laying up against his chest, had loaded up again and was shining and aiming at another one. He was set to pull the trigger when all of a sudden he's knocked flying through the water.

His first thought, he told me, was that he'd been run over by a boat. But knew that couldn't be possible, him being on the bottom. Then there's a giant set of gill plates sliding along the glass on his mask and his spear gun's being wrenched from his hands.

As his mask gets clear and he is no longer being pushed through the water, he can see a big shark, swimming slowly away from 'em, chewing up that big grouper that had been hanging by Charlie's chest. He's carrying Charlie's spear gun in his mouth like a dog carries a newspaper.

Charlie says he didn't take long getting back in his boat. Matter of fact he busted one ear drum going up so fast.

Charlie's tough though, he told me he felt he had to go back diving as soon as he could so he'd get over the fear.

He went back the next weekend and he's still diving now, so I guess he whipped that phobia.

Joe's Quick Thinking

Joe, another good customer of ours, told me that he and three of his buddies went out to dive on a rock in thirty-five feet of water off Alligator Point.

He said that when they got out there and anchored down that he wasn't feeling too good and decided to stay in the boat.

One of his buddies had forgotten his stringer, to put his fish on, so he got a piece of nylon rope, about twelve feet long, tied it to his B.C. and went diving.

This is what happened when they got back.

Joe says this guy with the long stringer has a habit of laying in the water as everyone else gets in the boat.

His practice is to put enough air in his B.C. to float 'em, hang on to the boat and chat.

This is what the guy was doing. He was talking to Joe while Joe was scrubbing the deck with a long handled scrub brush. The guy in the water had shot a big Sheephead while diving and had put it on the end of that twelve-foot rope, tied to his B.C.

Joe's scrubbing, the guy's yakking, when all of a sudden something snatches the guy's B.C., pulling 'em backwards in a jerk like someone grabbing your collar from behind and snatching you backwards, unaware.

"Hey Bill, cut that out," the guy in the water laughingly calls out. Then he looks up to see Joe and Bill standing in the boat looking back at 'em.

Joe says when he looks back behind the guy in the water and at the end of the twelve-foot rope, where the Sheephead used to be, there was a ten-foot shark with that black line in his mouth. The line attached to the guy's B.C.

The shark starts very slowly sucking up the line like a long string of spaghetti, and swimming up the rope to the guy in the water.

The guy in the water, very quickly wants to be, the guy outta the water. He's frantically trying to climb the boarding ladder but he hasn't taken his flippers off and keeps falling back in.

The shark's following that rope.

Joe and Bill have got the guy half in and half-out of the water by his tank and are trying to drag 'em over the stern but just can't do it.

The shark's almost to the end of the rope.

Luckily Joe uses his head, grabs his lethal scrub broom and whallops the shark on the top of the head just as he reaches the end of the rope attached to the now desperate guy half in and half out of the water.

The shark takes off, playing the line out of his mouth as he goes, minus the Sheephead.

They roll the guy now out of the water into the boat.

Joe says when they go diving now, the guy that stayed in the water is the first one out.

Amberjack

Bought the Ace in October of 1988. I've mentioned it before in other stories and how I got that great boat.

The Ace was thirty-two feet long, eleven feet wide with a six cylinder Perkins diesel, ice holds for two thousand pounds, bunks, stove and sink. We bolted two "bandits" on it and Don took us to an amberjack hole.

Now let me explain what a bandit is. I think bandit is a nickname derived from the one-arm bandit gambling machine, in that they both have a large arm or crank, that you turn by hand. The one on the gambling machine lets you gamble, The crank on our bandit lets you turn a big reel, with two hundred pound test on it, and bring in fish, sometimes little ones, sometimes huge ones, up from the bottom. Many times I've reeled 'em up two-at-the-time on grouper rallys. Most the time you reel 'em up to put on new bait cause something stole it. Now that I think about it our "bandit" has a lot in common with the gambling machine "bandit". You turn and turn and turn it, and most the time you come up empty.

Back to Amberjacks.

We cruise the forty miles offshore at about ten knots and anchored down on a place we named the "dragline".

Don told us that he'd caught some really big jacks here, up to sixty pounds, and lost many more they couldn't turn around.

I was new to this game so I hooked some cut bait on the bandit, let it down to fish and I picked up a bait rod and started catching live bait.

Nothing was going on. I caught a few bait fish but we didn't get a nibble on the big rigs.

Don got a mullet out of the ice box, one of the ones we brought to fry for supper, and hooked it whole on his stiff heavy grouper rod. He set the drag, and stuck it down in the rod holders built into the stern of the ACE.

I'm sitting in the captain's chair under the cab looking at Don's rod in the holder. I see the tip quiver once, and then jiggle two or three time real fast.

"Don, I think you're getting a bite," I'm pointing at his rod.

"You're right," he says as he runs the fifteen feet back to his rod.

Before he can get there his rod starts bending real slow, but steady and doesn't stop. As Don's grabbing his prize grouper pole from the holder, the rod tips almost at the water.

"Pow", the rod sounds like firing a thirty-ought-six as it breaks off above the reel. The line starts to scream out, goes a few yards and stops.

Don's now holding in his hands just the handle of the rod with the reel still bolted on the end. The line's taunt, disappearing straight down off the stern. Don's cussing and mad. He really looks silly. Reeling and reeling with no rod but yelling that there's something heavy still on the line but no fight.

I grab the gaff and go to the stern just as a huge fish slides quietly to the surface.

I sink the gaff in 'em and grunt and drag 'em over the side.

Don says that's an amberjack, a good one, and it must have killed 'em when he broke the rod cause he's never seen one come in without a fight.

It turns out he weighed seventy-six pounds.

We hooked some pigfish I'd caught, to try for bait earlier, on one of the bandits. I drop the sixteen ounces of lead and the live pigfish over the side and start paying off line.

The bandit's made of stainless steel pipe, two inches in diameter, bolted to the deck and side of the boat. It's got a flat, thick fiberglass rod about three feet long that looks like an axle spring on a car. The reel's a foot in diameter and lets out, or reels in, about two feet of line every time it goes around.

You're glad it's bolted to the boat.

You stand there letting that heavy mono pass through your hand as the bait heads for the bottom. When it gets there you reel up the slack with the bandit handle.

You feel the line, that you're loosely holding in your hand, start to get tight, slow but steady.

Then it gets really tight and the heavy bandit rod starts pointing down.

You jerk the heavy mono you're holding as hard as you can, holding any slack you get til you can take it up on the bandit reel and then you crank like mad.

You can't believe that's a fish on the end of your line. You know something's on there, but it must be a submarine. The heavy bandit rod's bent straight down towards the water. The giant reel on the bandit is squeaking and squealing as the two hundred pound mono's grudgingly pulled off.

Mark's got one on the other bandit, fighting 'em just like I am over here.

I finally start gaining line. You can put a lot of pressure on a fish with a rig like a bandit, especially when you gain experience and we learned quick.

You also learn that you can bring 'em to the boat too "green", not worn down enough. When you gaff a seventy to eighty pound fish like an amberjack and drag 'em in the boat too green, he'll beat you and the boat to pieces as he flops on the deck, sounding like a giant bass drum being beaten by two or three people, fast as they can, at the same time.

What a creature they are, amberjacks.

Nothing but muscle and tail. Built for power and speed like a living breathing torpedo with eyes, mouth and gills. Bronze on their backs, burnished silver on the sides with a horizontal dark line from nose to tail.

Great market fish, each one worth a buck a pound or more.

We got good at catching 'em. That ole hunter-gatherer instinct takes over a true fisherman's soul when the fish are in a "rally", when they bite everything you drop to 'em, as fast as you can drop it down.

You don't even look at 'em twice when you get 'em in the boat.

Get the hook out (there's a trick, use Jap Circle hooks and just twirl the line real fast) grab another pig fish, hook 'em on, in his back, throw 'em over, payout the line to get it down ninety feet and get ready.

Wham! I can't help but "ya hoooo" with a rebel yell as my bandit groans with the strain.

Mark hollers out like a drunken sailor as he sets the hook on one.

Don's raising hell at the stern, trying to fish two bandits at once.

The one thing we learned real fast was that you don't want rods and reels of the conventional kind if you were going to amberjack fish for money. Soon as we got back from our first trip when Don broke his rod we bought two more bandits for the stern corners of the boat, making a total of four bandits.

We could lay it to 'em when we could find 'em biting.

We learned the right bait. Pigfish, live pigfish. The amberjacks can't resist their little grunting noise they make when they're in distress, like when they've got a hook sticking through 'em.

Those Jap circle hooks, that we could remove quickly, they really paid off.

We learned how to gaff 'em efficiently, especially the big ones, over eighty pounds. You have to get behind 'em in the water with the gaff. What I mean is you've got to set that big piece of steel in their sides up close to their head and be going in the same direction the amberjack's swimming in. You can put the biggest one they grow in the boat by yourself. When they feel that gaff bite 'em they put on a burst of power with their tail like you wouldn't believe. If you're pulling in the same direction he is, and you're pulling up at the same time, that ole jockey boy amberjack, a hundred pounds or more, will literally jump in the boat.

Your deck mate better be ready to move cause a hundred pound jack hitting you in the back will knock you ass over tea kettle or break your leg.

We couldn't catch many jacks in the hundred pound class to start with. The month of December 1988, we lost twelve bandit rods, broken off where they bolt to the stainless pipe that's attached to the boat.

When somebody knew they had one they thought was eighty pounds or better, they'd call for someone to help 'em, if they didn't have a fish on themselves. The way you helped catch the fish was that the extra person would sit on the side of the boat with their shoulder and arm underneath the fiberglass flat bandit rod and help hold it up some, so it wasn't bent in such a drastic angle that it would break.

We heard they were making bandit rods out of Kevlar in Panama City and we ordered some to try out.

They wouldn't break. That's when we started catching eighty, ninety, hundred and ten pound fish with regularity. Benjamin Franklin's we called those amberjacks, hundred dollar fish. Fifteen, twenty of those sweet babies and we were happy boys.

I remember many times the deck of the ACE covered in fish. Blood thrown everywhere from those big fish thrashing on the deck. The ceiling over the deck spotted like a Dalmatian. All of us covered with slime and blood, smiling ear to ear, the fish on the deck sliding back and forth with the roll of the boat.

Gut 'em when they die. Lay 'em like big oak logs in the boxes and pack 'em in ice. The boat settling lower in the water, seeming more stable with a load in her belly.

A confident, victorious, satisfied feeling settles over the boat when the sun goes down and you've taken a bath on the back deck, mixed a good drink, put some mullet and onions on to fry for supper.

Life's good. Life's great.

Mother Nature's smiled on us again. That's why we get all we can, when we can, cause ole mom will have her frowny days aplenty.

My First Deer

I shot my first deer when I was sixteen years old and I wasn't even deer hunting.

Will and I had gone to Lake Talquin, thrown out a couple dozen decoys, crawled into an old standup blind and killed a morning. We sure didn't kill any ducks cause they weren't flying that day. The weather was too pretty I guess.

We picked up the decoys about 10 a.m. and started paddling back to the boat ramp to go home.

Almost all of Lake Talquin is surrounded by big time private land owners. The land is beautiful with gentle sloping hills coming down to the lake covered with old growth pine trees, oak and hickory. Most of the underbrush is shaded out. Prime deer country but you couldn't hunt it. Posted.

As we're paddling along the shoreline enjoying the scenery, kind of lazy like, with the warm sun shining in on us, a deer piles off the hill into the water right in front of the boat. Takes a quick look at us, and before I can grab my shotgun, jumps outta the water and tears off through the woods.

I'm right behind 'em.

The ole hunter – gatherer instinct has taken over.

I want that deer, hadn't ever killed one before and I want to bad.

This particular piece of land we're on (me and the deer), was a small peninsula sticking out into the lake. I could hear the deer running in the dry leaves and heard him stop when he reached the end of that little point of land.

Figuring the deer wouldn't want to swim across the entire lake he'd come back thru the middle of this little peninsula. So that's where I got, leaned up against an old pine tree and waited, listening.

Sure enough, here he comes, I can't see 'em yet, but I can hear 'em running hard, coming my way.

All I got is number 6 shot, high brass, for ducks, no buckshot, so I need 'em close and close he's going to be cause there he is 20 yards away, running like the wind and if I don't move he's going to run over me.

So here's what I do. I step over five feet, bring that old 12 gauge up to my should and let that deer have a full load of number 6's in the neck and shoulder from a distance of 10 feet, the deer is running right over the place I'd been standing seconds before.

Ass over tea kettle the old deer goes, like you'd chopped his front legs off, when the shot hits 'em. Sliding through the dry leaves and lying still, in a pile, dead as stone.

I can't believe it.

Two minutes ago I was paddling home from a sorry duck hunt and now I'm standing over my first deer, a young buck with two little nubs for horns, but a buck nonetheless. Proud as a peacock but a little nervous too cause he's an illegal deer (5 inch spikes is the law), and I'm on posted property. On top of that we've got to go back to a public boat ramp to load up and get outta here.

Nothing left to do but take the decoys out, put the deer in the bottom of the boat, dump the decoys on top and hope for the best.

Nerves raw as a bad sunburn when we reach the ramp, but the coast is clear. No game warden.

Believe me, the boat was loaded on the trailer in record time and up the road we go laughing and smiling like we'd robbed a bank and gotten away with it.

Calmed down and relaxed now, we pull in at a little country store to get some chocolate milk and a honey bun, happy as two larks on our good luck, bragging on our hunting skills as young boys do.

The calmness and relaxation evaporated instantly as a uniformed officer in his State of Florida, Fresh Water Fish and Game Commission marked vehicle pulls in the parking space beside us.

I'm already out of the car.

The officer gets out of his car, nods and speaks hello.

I nod and mumble back, looking back at the boat on the trailer piled high with decoys only to see a deer's leg hanging over the side of the duck boat.

My eyes pop out.

I want to run and hide.

I'm scared to look and see where the game warden is, but I hear him speak to the store owner as he goes in the door.

I finally get the nerve to look around and see the game warden headed for the bathroom at the back of the store.

As soon as he goes inside I jump back in the car, glance at Will, who's still as a statue, staring straight ahead, and back out of the parking space. Honey bun and chocolate milk forgotten, I try not to spin the tires in my haste.

Down the road we go, deer leg flapping in the wind, (I can see it in my rear view mirror) afraid to stop to tuck that leg back in, wanting to get as far away from that warden as possible.

Luck is with us that day cause we make it back to Will's house unchallenged. As soon as we calm down a bit, we go back to bragging what great and successful hunters we are.

Blood Lust

I call it blood lust. It may not be the right term, but that's what I call it.

It's that lust to kill things when you're young. I don't mean kill everything, like people, dogs and cats. I mean game, like fish, deer, turkey, quail, ducks, squirrels, rabbits and birds and I have to list birds here, cause most every young boy who grew up in the country or the suburbs of the south had a B.B. gun. And most every one of 'em tried to make all Jays, Cardinals, Thrushes and song birds, every single flying, flitting bird in the bushes extinct. I remember seeing little piles of every color you can imagine. Those little piles being bird feathers and those feathers attached to birds, bloody and battered and dead from the B.B.'s.

Forget the bike, forget the boat and poles, forget the girls.

Give me that B.B. gun, a shady wood, a full box of B.B.'s and a bunch of colorful song birds and I'm Ghengis Khan, George Patton, or Roy Rodgers. There's the enemy chirping and hopping around in those trees and I'm going to get 'em. Blood lust, young blood lust.

Most everybody grows out of that phase of it, and moves into another. Duck hunting, dove hunting, rabbits, things you can eat. They're bigger and you can hunt 'em with more sophisticated equipment; shotguns, rifles, double barrels, automatics, pumps. The blood gets pumping when the birds are flying hard and fast.

Get 'em while you can boys, it ain't like this everyday.

Deer and turkey hunting; that's what I'm talking about. Blood lust.

You see a buck on the right of way: You want to shoot it. And sometimes you do.

You see a turkey across some farmer's soybean field; you think about it all day. Figuring out your approach, how you're going to kill that bird.

Hogs, wild feral hogs, don't you just love 'em!?

All farmers hate 'em, there's no season, no limit, they run in bunches, "hot damn you can kill 'em all".

I think it's natural in males from the country and the woods; people who grow up outdoors.

It's probably why they draft young men and boys for the service, before they lose it and direct it to other animals. Human animals.

Somewhere you lose it. The blood lust, I mean.

Maybe when you've caught enough fish or shot enough deer and turkeys, piled up and picked enough dove and ducks, maybe then you start to lose it.

Maybe it's age.

Maybe you just change and start to see things different, start to wonder how all this stuff works, start seeing the pure beauty in nature and how it manages it's self, living, feeding, surviving, reproducing; despite us.

I don't know exactly when I lost mine, but I know exactly when I realized I'd lost it.

We were coming down the Spring Creek Highway in my old Toyota truck. Always carried an old pump shotgun under my seat for emergencies (snakes, thieves, deer or turkeys). A young turkey darted across the road in front of us, then another, then two, then four more. They all piled-up in the ditch on the east side of the road and when I say piled-up that's just what they did. Bodies touching, heads all in a wad like a buncha snakes looking at you.

I stop the truck, Mark dragging that ole pump gun out as we stopped.

Windows are open, we're at an angle facing right down the ditch. It's twenty-five yards, we got 'em dead to rights, all of 'em, can't miss.

Mark takes a bead.

"Don't shoot 'em", I say.

"What?" Mark says.

"Don't shoot 'em, let's just watch 'em".

That's when I knew I'd lost it.

Those birds were young, they hadn't learned yet. They were confused and they were beautiful. All stacked up in that ditch, feathers reflecting the sun. Looking at us in a curious way, blue and yellow flowers growing wild all around.

I know we could have killed 'em, probably killed 'em all. But I realized that I was enjoying it too much just watching, and seeing what they'd do.

Finally one darts into the woods.

Then another, then they're all gone.

Don't misunderstand, I'll still shoot a big gobbler in the spring. I still want to kill a shore-nuff big buck. I love to dove hunt. I commercial fish and crab and catch all I can. Nothing fires me up more than putting my net around a big bunch of mullet, but I don't waste anything. Nothing. I use it or it goes back in the ocean. If I kill it, I eat it. I appreciate and enjoy all of nature.

I've lost my blood lust.

Ben's First Bird

Ben and Clay are my two sons that I've carried mullet fishing, deer hunting, dove hunting, and rambling with me since they were old enough to go.

That was a point of contention sometimes with their mama, Mary Jane.

At this time, Clay was too little to go. Ben had been my "bird dog" for a couple of years and I had finally bought 'em an old Steven's, twenty gauge shotgun at the pawn shop. I had the stock cut down to fit his ten year old arms, gave 'em my Dad's old worn out camo hat, the kind that was round and looked like a soft bowl on his head, and took 'em to Wyatt Jackson's corn field.

We shot every Saturday at Mr. Jackson's. It was a tradition I'll never forget. We would meet under a huge live oak tree that sat on one side of the field, speculate on the bird population for that day, catch up on what everybody'd been doing that week, then hit the corn when the first birds started coming in the field.

That great old cornfield's a subdivision now, the fate of much of North Florida's prime game habitat. I still can't ride by there without getting that old mad-sad feeling, but back to Ben.

It was a gray, damp, cold day with the sky and everything around sorta black and white or gray. No color in the world on that day, no birds to speak of either.

Ben was lugging that old twenty gauge around, unloaded as I made 'em keep it at that time. I decided I'd quit trying to shoot at the few birds that were coming in and concentrate on Ben trying to kill one.

We set-up in the corn rows about twenty yards from an old bare limbed cherry tree, the kind of trees that seem to grow on every fence row of every corn field I've ever been in. Not too tall, all wrapped with briars at the base, skinny branches waving in the cold north wind. Just the kind of trees a dove likes to sit in and survey the field before he lights down to eat.

I know it's not "sportsman like" to shoot a dove off a limb but I wanted Ben to get the feel of aiming and shooting, the kick of the gun. If he could hit one sitting, we'd move on to flying birds next.

It wasn't long before a dove, making that sweet singing noise with his wings when he's stopping, lit in that cherry tree, bouncing up and down ever so slightly from his weight on that skinny limb.

Whispering, I tell Ben to stand up and shoot the dove.

At the very moment he's standing, putting the gun to his shoulder and taking aim, another single dove comes dropping from the sky between us and the bird on the limb.

"Shoot that one, Ben," I'm pointing to the bird flying in, "Quick, shoot 'em now."

BAM, that ole twenty goes off, that dove puffs feathers like somebody kicked a dandelion, folds up and falls to the ground.

My young son probably though his Daddy had gone crazy. I whooped, hollered "great shot" and took off through the corn, faster than any well trained retriever to get Ben's first bird.

I never forgot that look that a son can give his Dad when he knows he's made 'em proud of 'em and I only hope that Ben was as excited as I was.

Clay's First Bird

I can't help but think of my sons and the fun I've had with 'em growing up. I now realize that sometimes I was having more fun than they were
at the time, cause they had to go with me on these hunting and fishing
ventures. They might have wanted to do something else, but I gave 'em no
choice cause I enjoyed 'em so much. I think all in all they enjoyed it too.

This dove season we had had to rent a place to shoot birds cause they
had started building houses in our old corn field that we usually shot. We
rented an old corn field that had pines planted in it about four years ago.

We "made" us a bird field that year. First mowing between the rows
of planted pines, then harrowing the ground up til it was clean and "planting" wheat seed. Our "wheat field" had really paid off cause we had five or
six hundred birds feeding there each day and knew we were going to have
a great shoot on opening day.

We caught some mullet the day before the season opened, set up an
old gas cooker on the back of my pick-up in the shade of some pecan trees.
We sliced up a sweet onion, got out the mayo, some white bread, corn
meal, salt and pepper and had us a feast. May not sound good to you but if
you never sat under a good shade tree, eating hot mullet right outta the
grease, no plates, no forks, just bread, and mayo to set the sizzling mullet
on, wrapped up like a hotdog with a slice of sweet Vidalia onion to eat with
it, you've missed something.

Opening day of bird season was always special.

Seeing old friends, missing old friends.

Looking at new shotguns, bragging on old ones.

Talking about last year's shoots, wondering about today's shoot. What
time will the birds start to fly with it as hot as it is?

Wondering if the young boys on their first shoot will be able to hit
anything.

Well that was Clay's day.

He had that same twenty gauge that Ben used. Now that I think about
it he had that same ole camo hat, except now it had holes worn in it and the
age and sweat-yellowed cotton liner was showing through in places.

Clay and I went fifty yards or so from the tree line about three-thirty,
and tried to hunker down in the young pines. The field was made up of
three to four foot pine trees with all kinds of wild grasses and bushes growing
in two-foot wide narrow strips the length of the field. These strips were
separated by eight feet of clean gray-white dirt, tilled by the tractor and
covered with wheat. Row after row after row. Each dark green with the
young pines and highlighted with bright yellow fall flowers, small and

shaped like bells. Grasshoppers by the dozens would whirr-up all around you every time you'd brush a pine limb.

The day was dry, clear, hot. Typical early dove season.

The birds flew good. Shots rumbled all around the field as the birds came in to feed.

Clay would stand in the brush between the rows and fire that twenty gauge at birds I'd point out.

That day you didn't need to point 'em out. They were everywhere.

I'd shoot a few and then let Clay shoot, cause it's good to "kinda watch" a boy his age when the bird's are coming fast.

He'd load that side-by-side twenty up and shoot, load-up and shoot some more.

He shot down three or four birds real quick that afternoon. I say three or four cause on one I kinda helped with my twelve gauge. I was proud cause he was getting the hang of it and he was proud of himself, but I had still been pointing out the birds, making sure he was being safe with his gun, picking up the birds he'd shot down, taking care of 'em, watching out for 'em.

Anyway, he was out of shells, almost. He had one left and we were both real thirsty from all that good, salty mullet, so I told 'em to be careful, watch for birds and I'd leave 'em alone for a few minutes to go to the truck to get us some more shells and something to drink.

The hunt was perfect for a small boy to learn on. To hunt, by himself, for the first time. There weren't many people, the field was big, he couldn't sprinkle anybody with shot and they couldn't hurt him.

Occasional shots thumped out around the field as I made my way through the pines. I shot a couple of birds as I walked and heard Clay shoot his last shell but I couldn't see 'em or if he'd hit anything.

I picked up a couple of drinks, some #8's for Clay's twenty, and walked back to where he was in the field.

As I approached 'em, with his blond hair sticking out from under that old camo hat, framed against those pines and yellow flowers and that clear-blue October sky, I noticed he seemed to be standing a little taller, sort of cocky looking. I also noticed that he had that old 20 gauge in one hand, and in the other a dove.

I'll never forget that proud look on his face nor will I forget that feeling in my heart. I realized that more than just a boy learning to hunt birds by himself had happened that day. That a new phase in a young man's life and mine was beginning. That independence was coming on. That Daddy wouldn't always be needed to "point things out". That Daddy wouldn't always be there to point things out and to see that he was safe.

Anyway, if you haven't been there, you can't explain it to anyone.

STONE CRABS   CLAY MARSHALL LOVEL   11-8-99

Stone Crabs

We stone crabbed from 1989 to 1998. We used the ACE to run our traps. I've talked about the ACE many times and the many things we did with that boat. It was an all-purpose rig. We took one of the bandits off, replacing it with a hydraulic trap puller to bring the traps up. That puller had enough power to pull the boat over if it got hung up on a rock or to cut your arm off if it got caught in the trap line.

We rigged up about two hundred and fifty wire traps, got a good chart of the bottom of the area we wanted to crab, and started crabbing. It took us a couple of months to "tune-in" to where those big crabs liked to go, what to bait with, and when to go, but we eventually "got after 'em" pretty good.

Here's a typical trip.

The tide dictated when you got up in the morning. In Spring Creek, especially in the winter, the bay and the creek would go dry on norther's and full moon tides. Four o'clock was about the latest (if I was lucky), that I could sleep, a lot of times it was three.

Me and the crew, either Ben, Jake, Clay or Johnny, for a while Charlie, would meet at the boat, in the dark, and load her up. Most of the time only two of us went.

Usually we'd fueled up the night before, hand pouring up to a hundred gallons of diesel into the ACE's tank. We'd load ice, drinks and food after firing off that Perkins diesel to let her warm up.

Then came the bait.

That wonderful, beautiful, fragrant collection of grouper heads, mullet heads, backbones and heads of every kind of fish that swims in the Gulf of Mexico. Stingrays, catfish, garfish, shark. Split mullet carcasses, shad, dogfish. All the critters or pieces of critters, frozen, partly frozen, or you wished they were frozen, so they wouldn't smell so bad. Five to eight hundred pounds of thawing eyeballs and teeth to ride around for nine to ten hours, or however long it took to run the traps.

All the time you're loading bait you're watching the water fall from the tide going out, knowing you had to hurry to make it out the dark, twisty channel that leads out of Spring Creek.

You finally get loaded, tie the boat loose, turn on the spotlight and start picking your way out, sliding between oyster bars, shining up the channel markers. Everybody on the boat helping as a lookout to keep from running aground.

You don't need lights or lookouts to tell you when you've cleared the last channel marker and are headed offshore. The rise and fall of the boat from the outside swells tells you that. It also tells you what kind of day you're in for, as the bow rises and falls, higher and lower and the spray starts hitting the windshield. When you clear the Shell Point beacon and the spray is blowing all the way across the ten-foot wide stern, washing all that good bait-juice out the scuppers, you just grit your teeth, shake your head and start dreaming about how happy you'll be when you get back home tonight. You're going to earn your money today.

Two, two and a half hours of pounding and slamming and beating your way down to the east, you reach your first line of traps, each line's about three miles long, sometimes four. The boat's headed into the current while you pull, to give you slack in the line to hook it in the puller. The waves are breaking over the bow, water rushing around the deck. You're hooking the orange colored trap buoys with a six-foot gaff, trying to keep your balance and get the line in the puller, before it draws tight.

Hook the buoy.

Hook the gaff on the strut.

Pull the trap rope through the snatch block.

Wrap the rope around the puller wheel.

Turn on the hydraulic switch.

Watch the rope come tight out the back of the boat.

Watch, watch, watch, as the trap rises out of the breaking waves beside the boat.

Turn the puller off with one hand, as you swing the dripping, snapping, crawling with mad crabs, trap aboard with the other hand.

Unhook the latch that holds the traps shut.

Turn the trap over and shake the rock bass, octopus, hermit crabs and hopefully stone crabs out into a fish box.

Set the trap on the rail.

Stuff the bait-well full of fish heads.

Latch it back.

Make sure the rope's clear and throw the trap back overboard, always bait-well down.

Grab the gaff hook and catch the next buoy before it goes by the boat.

That was one, you say to yourself, only two hundred and forty nine more to go.

Fast as you hook 'em and dump 'em, bait 'em up and throw 'em back, the trap buoys come by the boat. The only break comes when you get to the end of the line of sixty or seventy traps.

What a break, and that's what you really do is break. While the boat's running back to get down-current of the next trap line you break claws off the stone crabs, throwing the healthy live crab back overboard to grow a new claw or claws for next season. What other resource or animal do we know of that we can catch, take the most desirable meat off of, and turn it loose to regenerate that meat to harvest again next year. Sure can't take a ham off a hog and turn 'em loose.

Back to breaking crabs.

If you had a good blow out of the south or southwest during the five or six day "set" that your traps were in the water, it's not unusual to have three or four boxes of stone crabs to "break". All the crabs in the box are capable of really putting a hurt on you if you let one catch you. The big stone crabs, with claws that weigh half-a-pound or more can crush anything they get ahold of, especially fingers. If one does get ahold of you, all you can do is go ahead and break his claw off, cause that's the only way he'll turn loose. Most people think you can only break one claw off the crab, but that's not true. The law says the claw's got to be two and three quarters inches long to harvest. Most the time the crab's only got one claw that size, his crusher claw, the cutter claw being somewhat smaller, but on really big crabs, both claws are legal size and we get 'em both.

There's not much spare room on the big deck of the ACE when you're pulling traps. Bait is stacked on the stern, torn and damaged traps stacked somewhere else. Round, orange, plastic baskets, that hold seventy pounds apiece are set all around on the deck with different fish or crabs in 'em. Rock bass in one, grunts in another. Octopus to send to New York are separated out, along with slick skin toads or blowfish. Large stone crab claws in still another basket, medium claws have their own basket too. The six-foot waves, that occasionally break over the side of the boat, keep all of the catch in their bright little baskets washed clean and shiny.

The man running the boat's yelling over the diesel, wind and waves, that the next line is coming up so you stop breaking claws and get set-up to pull the next line.

The last trap is always a pretty thing. It signifies that the hard part's over. The day's work's not over by any means, but the back breaking, trap pulling, bait stuffing part's done with. The two or three hour trip back to the dock is filled with things to do.

Finish breaking claws.

Grade out the rock bass, small, medium, large, all bring different prices.

Skin out the blowfish tails.

Catch up all the octopus that have crawled all over the boat during the day.

Ice down all the fish.

Wash out all the bait containers.

Scrub the whole boat down with bleach and salt water cause there's mud, blood, grass, bait and seaweed everywhere, including the ceiling.

You're finally back to the dock, maybe a little before dark if you're lucky.

Now to cook the claws.

You can't ice stone crabs when they're "green" or uncooked. You can't even store 'em overnight "green". They'll stick to the shell if you do and you can't get the meat out. So you have to cook 'em as soon as you get in. Fifty pounds at the time is what our cooker would handle. If we had a good day and caught two hundred pounds that's four cookings.

Get twenty gallons of water to a rolling boil.

Put fifty pound of claws in.

Wait for it to come back to a full boil and cook 'em for ten minutes.

Take 'em out, chill 'em in an ice slush, pack 'em in wax cartons.

All the time we're cooking claws, we're packing fish and octopus.

When the last cooking's done, dump the pot of hot water, scrub it, and the cooking room down.

It's well after dark now. Check the lines on the ACE, go up and take a shower and go to work in the restaurant.

That's about it and I get tired just thinking about it.

Instinct

Instinct.

Natural instinct.

I think it's being bred out of us.

Naturally.

I think we're civilizing instinct right out of our culture.

I think we're losing the inborn abilities to hunt and gather. Abilities that all of us once had to have to survive.

I think some people have even lost their knowledge of where food comes from. Much less how to catch, grow or kill it and prepare it to eat.

I point to the anti-hunting groups and their growing popularity.

I point to the non-concern that everyone displays, or doesn't display, over the plight of the small farmers in this country.

I point to the net ban in Florida that took the fish from the working people, that need these fish to eat and make a living from. And gave them to the sports and recreational fishermen to only play with.

I hear people complaining about deer hunting and dove hunting while they're cutting up and eating a medium rare steak.

"Don't cut the trees down, but don't let me run out of toilet paper".

"Why don't you have mullet?" someone will ask.

It's been blowing a Northeaster for two weeks, and the person complaining about not having fish voted for the net ban that took all our gear away.

They believe everything comes from the grocery store.

Publix, Winn Dixie, Food Lion, Piggly Wiggly.

Everybody wants everything, all the time, no toil, no sweat, no blood, no challenge.

Temperature between 68 and 72.

Cold and hot running water.

Soft beds.

Hard beds.

Beds that are soft in some places, hard in others.

3,552 T.V. channels plus ESPN 1 and 2.

Garbage pickup.

Garbage delivery.

Mail, paper; UPS delivers to your door.

Cars with warm seats and cold air.

Three hot meals a day plus snacks.

Health insurance.

Burial plan.

Retirement.

Social Security.

Pills for too slow, pills for too fast, pills to wake up, pills to fall asleep.

Instinct, what's that? Who needs it?

Don't need it anymore!

Maybe just enough to run from a vicious poodle or an IRS agent, but not much.

Some of us still need it.

Some of us still have it and have to have it to get by.

Maybe if we can retain our instinct long enough, we can rent a building next to Wal-Mart and give lessons.

Down In The Dumps

Been down in the dumps all day. Black ass, the blues, what ever you want to call it.

No reason to be, just have.

Tried to talk myself out of it, going over all the good things in my life and there's plenty of 'em, but that didn't work.

Cooked lunch with the boys down at the fish house. The sausage wasn't worth a damn so that didn't help me perk up.

Called a few of my buddies but they sounded as bad as me.

Must be the weather.

Decided to go pull some crab traps. The bay always makes me feel better, puts me in my place, shows me how small and insignificant I am, specially my worries and my cares.

That helped.

Don't know why but it always does.

To see all the seabirds hunting for their daily bread, leaning against the cold hard wind. To shake the poor ole crabs out of the trap, them just hunting for some food, makes me realize that I don't matter much. They don't care. The crabs wouldn't even notice if I fell out of the boat and drowned right there. Might make life easier for 'em, as much food as I would make.

I could fall overboard right here and as soon as the ripples died away from my splash the wild world wouldn't know the difference.

The birds would sing.

The crabs would feed, the fish would jump, the sun would set the same time it always does.

The tide would fall and rise its schedule with the moon. People that didn't know me would laugh and party without a care.

We don't amount to much, us people don't. Only we think we're special.

We're not, except to our immediate loved one, and with time, they forget.

The bay always does this to me.

Puts me in my place, makes me feel better by making me feel small, microscopic, unimportant, just a natural part of things with my time and place limited.

I better enjoy my time and place, I never know where or when it's going to end.

I feel better now.

My Boys

The rain finally quit today.

It rained all day long Sunday, I mean it stormed, the ground was soaked, it was under water.

I was working in my room – cleaning up, straightening up – doing some laundry.

Happened to look over at my son's house across the street from the restaurant – Ben my oldest son and Clay my youngest; (Ben will be 25 next month, Clay 20), they came walking outta the house.

I was struck, I guess that's the word, as I watched 'em come walking across the road, walking across the parking lot.

I couldn't believe they were as old as they were, they seemed like they were still my boys, my little boys, but there they were, grown men; almost grown men.

A feeling of pride welled up in me.

Hard to describe.

Knowing that not only was I looking at my two sons that were grown and moved out, I was looking at my two best friends. Two people that I feel happy to be around, I feel comfortable to be with, I feel proud of, proud of everything they've done.

I just wish that every parent, every person who ever had a child, could be as fortunate as I am, as my wife Mary Jane and I are, to have two children that we love so much, that we would do anything for and we feel like would do anything for us and always have, anything we ask 'em. If all the parents in the world could have two children that they loved and the children loved them as much as we do, the world would be a wonderful place.

I'm proud of my wife and boys.

I'm proud of my whole family.

All I ever want to do is make my family proud of me.

MY FIRST SPRING GOBBLER   CLAY MARSHALL LOVEL   7-20-99

My First Spring Gobbler

I'll never ever forget the first Spring Gobbler I shot.

Johnny Rivers and I went down to Black Gum Swamp well before daylight one warm, April morning.

J.R. had called and hunted turkeys all his life and had shot many fine gobbler turkeys, but I had yet to hear one answer the yelps of the hen and come thundering through the woods.

We set up beneath an old oak tree that was a full 6 feet in diameter, growing out of a little high place in the swamp. Johnny hooted like an owl once or twice and we thought we heard an answer way in the distance, but it was hard to hear over the drone of ten thousand mosquitoes. When Johnny yelped once or twice we knew we heard a turkey gobble and he was coming to check us out. Johnny got on one side of that huge old oak tree and I got on the other. Being back to back that way we figured we'd have 'em covered when he made his move to the tree.

Try to picture this.

A dark, double canopy Florida swamp at gray daylight. Everything gloomy and in shadow, all grays and blacks with the only color the green of the palmettos that grew in round clumps when they could get enough daylight to grow.

Ten million hundred thousand skeeters buzzing like electric shavers all around your head with five hundred perched on each leg, 10 on your nose that you can see, must be fifty thousand on each ear and you can't move a muscle cause that turkey will see you and the game will be over.

All you want to do is slow down your heartbeat before it jumps out of your chest, cause that old gobbler's coming. He's announcing his approach with every breath he takes. Johnny can't even finish his yelps before that big turkey shakes all the remaining leaves out of the trees with a gobble that's louder and louder every time he takes a step.

You ain't seen 'em yet but there's no doubt he's coming.

His gobbling is so loud that you know he must be on top of you and your heart is about to blow your eardrums out, you glimpse a flash of bright orange or red in the black gloom in front of you. Then nothing. Then that earthshaking gobble rings out again and you know he's right there.

Then a glimpse of a blue-white head.

Gone.

Then the whole bird as he comes from behind a tree, to go behind another tree.

There ain't no skeeters buzzing, there ain't no skeeters biting. There ain't no morning dampness and chill, there ain't no bills to pay, obligations to fulfill or problems in the world.

There's just that turkey.

Up comes the 12 gauge to the shoulder.

Out comes the turkey from behind a tree only to disappear from sight like magic before you can pull the trigger.

Where'd he go? Where'd he go?

How could he do that?

You're still sighting down the barrel, only six skeeters on your nose now, gun getting heavy. Heavy, but you can't move now, he's right here on me, he can't have slipped away.

The old gobbler steps up out of a dry creek bed I didn't even know was there twenty yards away.

BAM!

Down he goes flopping and a flapping.

Up I jump, following my shot to grab that big gobbler before he can get away. Like I was shot-out-of-a-cannon I come off the ground. Well at least my body does. Unbeknownst to me, my feet must have fell asleep in the long, still wait and they don't move at all! It's like my body's flying and my feet are nailed to the ground. All I do is get up off my butt and fall flat on my face.

I tried to get up real fast, before Johnny sees me, but he came boiling around from the other side of the tree laughing so hard I thought he would fall.

He didn't know if I'd killed the turkey or the turkey had killed me. But I had killed that old gobbler, ten-inch beard, inch and a quarter spurs, eighteen pounds of beautiful Florida swamp turkey.

I don't know what Johnny was saying to that bird that day. Whether he was challenging 'em to fight or calling 'em over to make love, but whatever it was it sure had 'em excited. It had me excited too cause he never missed a breath gobbling. He must have gobbled fifty times on his way to us.

You know, the skeeters got bad again after we picked that old bird up off the ground, our hearts beating back to normal, our adrenaline down. Heading home.

Wonder why that was?

GFC

A good friend of mine gave me permission to go turkey hunting on a twelve hundred-acre piece of property he leased to deer hunt on.

The property is located about halfway between Ecofina and Lamont. I had trouble finding it even with his good directions and a map he drew for me. It's truly in the middle of nowhere. Typical north Florida flat lands, planted in pine trees of various ages, hardwood and gum hammocks with logging roads dividing up the property in large blocks.

I found plenty of turkey sign most everywhere I looked. Picked the place I thought most promising, called my buddy Johnny Rivers and we set things to go try for a bird on the following morning.

I'd found everything I needed. The property, the turkey sign, a good hunting partner, but the one thing I couldn't find anywhere I looked, was a hunting license. I tried every bait and tackle shop in three counties, but it was late in the season and everyone was out of licenses. I started to call J.R. and cancel the trip but decided that as remote as the area was, I could get away with going hunting one time without a license.

Here's what happened.

Johnny met me a little before six a.m. in Wacissa to follow me to the property. I made one more attempt at the Wacissa store to obtain a license, but they were out too. I even laughingly told the store owner I was going to use him as a witness if I got caught by the wardens to prove that at least I'd tried to do right.

We drive ten miles down a dusty dirt road, find the right gate, unlock it and purposely pull our trucks around a bend in the road to hide 'em from the highway. I lock the gate back for good measure.

By the way, I never did tell Johnny that I didn't have a license, it didn't seem to be that important.

I owe Johnny three or four turkeys. He's called that many up that I've ambushed laying up ahead of where he's calling from. Some of the gobblers I've killed were real prize winners and I wanted to pay him back by putting 'em in a hot spot.

He and I moved down the road about two hundred yards from where we'd parked and I showed 'em all the turkey sign in the road. Even in the pre-dawn darkness you could see the tracks and where the ole gobbler had drug his wings in the dirt while he was strutting.

We hooted a few times like an owl, trying to get the birds to gobble back, but no response. It's starting to gray up as it does before the sun comes up and we discussed what to do. I told Johnny to go ahead and set-up on these birds as it was the best sign I'd seen on the whole place. I told him I'd go back past where we'd parked and hunt in the clear cut and that's what I did. I back tracked the way we'd come and eased along the edge of the swamp.

I found a little grove of gum trees that jutted out into the clear cut, set-up and yelped a few times just as the sun peeked over the horizon.

No response. No gobbling, no clucking, nothing but a pretty morning in the woods.

I got to thinking about all the things I needed to do that day, being it was soft crab season and we had a pile of traps to run and a bunch of crabs to pack up and ship out. The turkeys didn't seem to be interested in getting shot that day so I decided to ease my way back to the truck and leave.

I've got all my camo gear still on, full face mask, gloves, camo jump suit and hat. I'm easing along the wood line looking for turkey tracks and picking up pieces of chipped flint and broken spear points that have been uncovered when they plowed and planted the new pine seedlings. It's cool and kind of misty with a little ground fog coming up as the sun warms the earth. The cardinals and wrens are chirping and singing. Everything's peaceful and serene, a great day to be outdoors.

Then I look up towards the trucks, and my heart jumps up into my throat.

Bent over the side of my pickup, rummaging around in the back of it, is a man with a jacket on that has in big, bold yellow letters, one foot high, G.F.C., which I know stands for Game and Fish Commission.

I take two quiet steps to my right to melt into the thick briars and gums growing between the rows of planted pines.

I can't believe it. Out here in the middle of nowhere this warden's found us and decided to check us out. Me with no hunting license, no turkey stamp, no nothing but a violation ticket waiting.

The man hasn't seen me or heard me as I watch him look through the windows of my truck and then check Johnny's truck out.

I decide I'm in no hurry to receive my ticket so I just stand real still and watch.

The man moves to the side of the trucks and starts studying the ground and looking up the road the way Johnny and I had gone before daylight. He takes a few slow steps in that direction, stops and studies the ground some more, tracking us just like we do the turkeys. He's in no hurry. Looking, listening, he takes a few steps, stops again.

I'm the turkey now and I know how one must feel when he sneaks up behind the hunter and finds out that's no turkey hen calling to 'em.

The man's slowly moving down the road in Johnny's direction and is about fifty yards ahead of the trucks.

I'm looking around for the other warden, they usually travel in pairs, and I'm looking for their vehicle and I can't find either one.

He's still slowly moving away.

I step out of my hiding place, staying close to the wood line and slowly, quietly, walk toward the trucks. I'm trying to not look like I'm sneaking along in case the other warden's hiding there at the trucks, but I'm being as quiet as possible, walking slow with all my camo still in place.

I reach the trucks.

I sit down on the back bumper waiting to see if the second warden pops out like a jack-in-the-box to get me.

All's quiet.

I take off my hood and gloves.

Still quiet.

I peek around the driver's side of my truck and I can still see the bright G.F.C. letters easing down the road, maybe now a hundred yards away.

I go sit back down on the bumper.

Maybe there's hope.

I nonchalantly remove my camo jump suit, roll it up and put it in the truck bed.

I peek around the truck again.

He's further down the road now, still studying out tracks.

I ease up to the passenger side of the truck (he can't see me on that side) and gently unlock the door. I stick my old twelve gauge in the truck and unload it as quietly as I can and I put it behind the seat (No officer, I wasn't hunting, I was just scouting). I put all my camo gear behind the seat too, walk back to the tailgate and peek out again.

I can still see 'em but he's further down the road and about to go around a slight curve that will put 'em out of sight of my driver's door.

I make a decision.

If he gets around that curve and another warden doesn't show up, I'm going to leave 'em with Johnny. I know Johnny Rivers is going to give 'em an earful about messing with his turkey hunt by walking into his set-up.

I peek around again and I can't see anybody.

My heart starts thumping hard as I unlock my driver's door as quiet as I can. I open the door just wide enough to get in and hold it slightly open cause I don't want the door latch to "click".

The engine seems to sound so loud as I crank it up.

I've got to do a three-point turn to go out and my heart's really racing now.

I get turned around and drive slow and natural up to the gate, knowing that second warden is going to jump out any second. I start seeing in my mind that warden that's down the road, running as fast as he can back up to where we were parked, cause he hears my truck and it's all I can do not to run up to the gate, snatch it open and haul ass, but I don't. I unlock the padlock, walk the gate open, prop it where it won't fall shut, get back in my truck, pull through the gate, get out again and close the gate.

When I get the chain around the post and the padlock through the chain I can't help but half-run back to the truck and get in. Still seeing in my mind that warden racing down the road like a world class sprinter to stop me before I leave.

I shift into low gear and let out the clutch and pull out onto the hard road, still easy and calm.

I shift to second gear and restrain from stomping on the gas.

I'm still looking for that second warden or their vehicle and I haven't seen either one.

When I shift into third gear I can't help but turn that V8 loose. That ole standard transmission, 305, GMC will go when you get into it, and I'm into it now. When the pavement runs out and the road turns to crushed limerock, I'm snatching her into fourth gear at about eighty, rebel yelling and it looks like a giant, white tornado behind the truck from all the limerock dust I'm sucking up. I can't believe my bad luck, can't believe my good luck. Hope Johnny won't be too mad at me leaving The Man with him.

I sure know what it feels like to be a turkey now. I wonder if those turkeys feel as good as I do now, when they give me the slip.

I bet they do.

CORMORANT

CLAY MARSHALL LOVEL   9-5-99

Cormorant

Caught a cormorant in one of my stone crab traps once.

He was drowned, of course. He had somehow found his way through the funnel just like a crab.

After the bait I guess.

He had a band on his leg so I saved it and sent the number in to the Feds.

I got a reply back that said that he had been banded as a fledgling on an island in Canada in June of the year I found him in the trap.

I found that to be amazing.

A creature that had been born in June, grew up to adult size, flown 2000 miles by some unknown instinct to the Gulf of Mexico and had found his way into my trap in twenty feet of water in November of that same year.

It's amazing that wild creatures mature and travel the distance that they do in the time span that they do it in.

I guess they have to grow up and live fast.

They sure can die fast.

Set Nettin'

There was always an air of excitement, anticipation, maybe a dab of apprehension, every time we'd back the ACE as close as we dared get, to the breakers right on the dry beach of Dog Island.

Sometimes a swell would set the ACE down hard, it's keel slamming the bottom, and Johnny'd know to throw the anchor, tied to the end of the net, as far towards the beach as he could get it.

I'd already have the boat in forward, moving away from the shallow dangerous shoreline when I'd hear the splash from 'em throwing it out.

We were fishing pompano. Straight setting two shots of net, two hundred yards each, four and a half inch stretch monofilament, perpendicular to the shore. We had to get the ends of both nets as close to the beach as possible cause the pompano like to run along where the waves are breaking and churning up the bottom, digging up the sand fleas that pompano love to eat.

One hour soak time, was how long we'd set 'em and then take 'em up.

Every take-up an adventure.

Sometimes the net would be completely empty. Nothing. Not a fish.

Sometimes there'd be a little of everything.

Sharks, bonnet heads, blacktip, lemon, sand sharks.

Big speckled trout. It takes a big fish to gill off in four and a half inch mesh.

Sheephead. Stingrays. Damn blue crabs and horseshoe crabs wadding up enough webbing around their claws and legs to make a cast net out of.

Once we were sitting there, letting the nets soak, and as we were watching, one whole two hundred yard long net, with anchors on both ends, bends into a sharp vee about the middle and the whole damn net start moving down the shoreline, dragging anchors, buoys and all. We didn't know what we were in for as we chased the offshore end of the net down. All we knew for sure was that some huge, huge sea creature had swam into the net and was dragging the whole thing with 'em, wherever he was going.

When Johnny drug the end of the net over the stern and we started frantically tripping net on the boat, we were both a little bit more than nervous over what kind of battle we were going to have to fight when we got to this monster that was stealing our pompano net.

Lucky for us whatever it was finally pushed the corkline down and went on.

We never saw what it was, really didn't want to.

I remember one time when we were pitching the end out close to the beach and as I went to put the boat in gear, the pompano went to jumping and skipping all out from under the boat, hopping like a bunch of grasshoppers, getting us real excited.

I think we caught almost a hundred head that set.

At four dollars a pound and almost two pounds a piece, not a bad catch.

Pretty fish, pompano are. Sleek, no teeth. Oblong shape, silver sides with dark gold bellies, big eyes, big bucks. We got twenty dollars a dinner for 'em in the restaurant, one fish to the plate. I loved 'em.

Loved fishing for 'em. We'd make one or two special trips each year to the West end of Dog Island just to try for 'em in late April or early May.

First set right before daylight. The last set we'd take up at dark. Ten on one set, two the next set, twenty-five the third time. We had finally got us a pattern worked out with the tides and the fish. We were doing better every year.

We'd also figured out a way that just two of us could strike, take-up and operate that thirty-two foot boat, the ACE. We rigged a regular cane fishing pole to the gearshift lever, the pole twenty feet long, so I could shift it in and outta gear from the stern while taking up net with Johnny. Oh we'd get excited to see those silver-gold fish coming over the stern. I loved to be picking a frisky, fat pompano out, Johnny working on another one, with two or three more, hung in the net, still in the water, swimming hard but going nowhere, caught.

Sometimes if the pomps seemed to be in the net from the deep end to the shoreline we'd just trip the net, fish and all on the boat, and clear 'em out. The thought of one or two of 'em falling outta the net while we're trying to clear the fish one at a time, too terrible to bear. We wanted 'em all.

That's all history. Done for. We can't do that anymore. They gave all the pompano to the tourists, and the sports fishermen. Pompano aren't food anymore. They're play toys.

We sure enjoyed it.

I haven't had a pompano in my hands since '95, but I can remember what they felt like, what they looked like. I can also remember the smiles they brought to our faces as we picked 'em from the net, one after another after another after another.

SOFT SHELL CRABS   CLAY MARSHALL LOVEL   G- -99

Soft Crabs

Nature is amazing. The Old Maker about out did Himself when He put the Blue Crab together.

We went into the soft crab business to help keep our fish house and restaurant afloat after the net ban in 1995. What we've learned about 'em in the four years we've been catching and shedding 'em is truly amazing.

Soft shell crabs are the same ole hard-shell blue crab, that we've all seen at the beach. They become a soft shell crab when they shed their shells, or molt, as they call it in more formal circles.

We deal mainly in female crabs. Adolescent females to be more exact.

The way we catch these adolescent females or "peelers", as we call 'em, is to put two or three big, mature, horny male crabs in a little peeler trap, a smaller version of a regular crab trap but made with smaller mesh wire. These male crabs, believe it or not, do some kind of dance in the trap. They stand up high on their six legs with their big claws out, stretched wide to their sides like they were going to defend a basketball goal. They have their flat swimmer fins crossed behind their backs and they're rubbing 'em together like you would if you were trying to build a fire by rubbing two sticks together.

Evidently they make a scent or a sound that the peelers tune into and come into the trap for a "visit".

The males get the peelers close at hand and run over and grab the little crab, maybe three inches long, and tuck her up underneath his body, holding her there with four of his legs. The little adolescent peeler is right side up, facing the same way the male crab is. She's just being carried around by the male who's waiting for her to shed her shell.

We come along, most everyday, and shake all the crabs out of the trap. The males are all toting peelers underneath 'em. If we're lucky and the crabs are running good, there's a bunch of what we call "ladies in waiting", or extra peeler crabs that have answered the male crab's call and are waiting their turn.

By the way, the big male crabs are called "Jimmy's". It seems like the bigger the "Jimmy" the better. The traps that have those old "Jimmys" that have barnacles on their backs and grass growing underneath the points of their shells, attract larger numbers of peelers to the trap. The best we can tell it's the end of their life cycle to carry and breed those females cause we've noticed that they don't even eat the fish heads we feed 'em when the peelers are running good.

We take the "peelers" each day and bring 'em back and put 'em in our tanks in the "crabhouse" and wait for 'em to molt. The big "Jimmy" crabs we put back in the trap to call in more peelers.

I've watched the shedding process ten thousand times and I never cease to wonder at it.

The little three to four inch peeler first cracks open at the back of her shell where the top shell joins the bottom half. She begins to bulge out at the back, looking much like somebody's beer gut hanging over their belt with their shirt too short. She's still swimming free in the tank at this point but that's soon to stop. Once her new body gets well out the back of her shell she can't swim and is totally vulnerable to all other creatures that live in the sea, including other crabs that aren't in the molting stage.

That's where the "Jimmy" crab earns his keep in the wild. He's carrying this defenseless crab with 'em, keeping all the predators away while she's soft.

But he gets a reward.

When the adolescent peeler finishes shedding her shell she's an adult female crab with eggs and an egg bag and that's when the Jimmy gets to fertilize her eggs.

He turns the now soft shell crab over, still carrying her with his legs and fertilizes her eggs and continues to carry her around until her shell gets hard and she can swim and defend herself with her claws.

She's almost double the size she was before she molted.

When she's coming out of her shell all her points on her shell are doubled over, tucked inside her old one. She's as soft or softer than a wet sponge. She immediately starts absorbing great amounts of water and stretching her body out like a balloon.

In our tanks we let the now soft crab stay in the water for about an hour to grow bigger and for her shell to firm up enough for her to support her own weight. We can't leave the soft crab in the water too long cause within two to three hours her shell will get as hard as crab shells get, but if we take her out of the water her shell will never get hard. It won't firm up in the air. We can pack her in wet hay and she'll stay alive for almost a week in a wet, moist and cool environment, and she'll stay soft.

Crabs are meant to stay with us on this earth. They were given an ability to survive that I don't know if it is equaled in many creatures.

When their eggs are fertilized and their shells get hard, if they find themselves in a bad environment for egg bearing, such as too cold or too hot water, water that's too salty or too fresh, or they happen into an area that's polluted, they can stop the gestation process at will, and for as long as they want to. They can swim for a week or wait on the right conditions and start the process up again. They can stop it again if need be til they're satisfied that their eggs can hatch.

It's hard to eliminate any animal with reproductive ability like that. Even though man seems bound and determined in some cases to do just that with his pollution and destruction of habitat.

Fenholloway River's a good example.

So the next time you enjoy a nice fried soft crab dinner, think about what a miracle of nature you have before you on your plate. Enjoy it, knowing that you wouldn't have this fresh delicious seafood if the waters where it came from weren't pure. It is a delicate creature, ancient as the dinosaur, primitive, but a sensitive product of a good healthy environment, tasting of the sea and the earth and born with an instinct to survive forever, as long as man doesn't mess everything up.

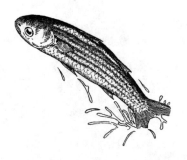

Riverbluff

I may have mentioned before that we bought some property in Middle Georgia.

It's really special.

I was smitten by it the moment I stepped on the place. Spent a year of my life scheming and plotting and selling everything I owned to get it. Without the support of my family, we'd have never got it, but we did. I feel like some ancestor of mine must be buried on the place somewhere, that's how hard that land grabs me, pulls on me. Talk about love-of-the-land, I've got it now, we've all got it.

We're mighty proud of it and here's why.

It's located in a small farming county of five thousand people. The little country restaurants that are scattered around, serve fresh local vegetables, homemade "nanner" pudding or peach cobbler with fried chicken, or ham. The general stores sell everything from groceries, fresh meats, home cured bacon and sausage, to crickets, bullets, worms and clothes. Most business is done with a handshake and a smile. We can trade mullet for steaks, vegetables, whiskey and beer.

The property itself is on the Flint River, almost two thousand feet of it. The last set of rock shoals to go all the way across the river make the river roar like the ocean, keeps almost all the boat traffic stopped and draws fish like a magnet.

There's a cabin perched high on a bluff overlooking the river. It's almost two hundred feet at an unwalkable angle up to it. When you walk into the cabin and out on the porch, you can see for about twenty miles and you can't see another house or road, just trees and sky. In the summer you're living in a tree house cause the land falls away so sharp that the porches are up in the very tops of big white oak trees and hickory trees with dogwood and beech mixed in. It's so green when you look outside that you can't stay inside.

The cabin itself is rough-cut local pine, board and batten, hardwood floors, big brick fireplace that draws like a vacuum cleaner and a tin roof that puts you to sleep like a drug when it's raining. It's the warmest, most comfortable, most beautiful place you'll ever go when you look at the inside and outside together.

There's a spring on the property that runs through the worst droughts, clear, cold water.

There's a waterfall in one of the ravines in a creek that looks like North Carolina, with the big rocks and gurgling water.

We've got fifty acres of planted pines that are twelve years old and

173

will give us a little old-age money if we grow 'em out right.

The other hundred acres, for a total of a hundred and fifty two, is steep-sided deep ravines, totally covered in old-growth hardwoods, a few big long leaf pines and every other kind of tree and bush that grows in Georgia. Wild plums, black berries, osage orange grow where the light's right. The bottoms of the ravines are like tropical rain forests in the summer with double canopy, even triple canopy in some places. Always cool and damp even in the middle of the day. Each ravine has its own personality, its own type vegetation and trees. Some ravines are wide and flat at the bottoms, others you come down one side and start straight up the other, just a steep, sharp slice in the earth.

There's a three-acre pond that backs up into the woods down on the flood plain, close to the river. Bream, bass and catfish in it, beavers and otters too.

Game, birds, animals, we got 'em. Everything you can name. Doves, ducks, deer, turkey, squirrels, rabbits, coyotes, fox, bob cat, chipmunks, quail, rattlesnakes, water snakes, coons, possum, hummingbirds, all your song birds, geese, we got it all and then some.

Wake up in the morning, put your feet on the floor and there's a deer, or many deer, bucks, does, yearlings, fawns, looking at you through the window.

Mary Jane and I stood on the front porch at dusk-dark one evening and watched and listened to a whole flock of turkeys fly-up and roost not fifty yards from the cabin. We sat on the porch the next morning and listened to 'em cluck, yelp and putt til ten o'clock, like a bunch of old women gossiping.

Ben, my oldest son, killed one of the biggest eight point bucks anybody'd ever seen, the first year we had the place. We knew the land and the ancient ones had accepted us, when it gave that big buck to us.

Clay, our youngest, caught his first bass, a fighting, jumping Shoal Bass, standing in the middle of the river, casting ultra light rigs, water roaring around his legs, me right beside 'em. Stuffing the fish down his jeans pocket, cause we didn't have a stringer and wanted to fish some more.

There are almost too many special places on this property to name.

The promontory. A big rock point, fifty feet above the river that juts out almost into it.

Turkey trot road. A steep beautiful road that curves its way down to the river, completely canopied, with carpets of wild ferns growing down almost vertical banks.

The burial grounds. A powerful place like the Promontory. Who's buried there, when? We know they're Indians, but what Indians, what era?

I think they're ancient. Older than the mound builders, the Indians that lived just hundreds of years ago, not thousands.

We don't bother the graves. Wouldn't dream of it. No matter what treasures they might yield. They like us and we like them, and we respect 'em.

We're at complete peace up there, no people, no sounds of people, watching the deer, catching fish outta the river, working on the roads, maintaining the pines, putting up deer stands, planting bird fields.

Money can't buy it. As hard as we work just to maintain our debts and obligations, no one in the family would sell Riverbluff for any price. There's not enough money in the world. You can't replace this property anywhere. It's priceless. Not for just its natural beauty and wildlife, but also for the power it emits, the aura of peacefulness and oldness. We say we "own" this land, but no one really "owns" anything. We're all just borrowers, fortunate enough to be the custodians of this special place we call Riverbluff. A place you can only imagine in your dreams.

I feel like I'm dreaming every time I'm up here.

He Gobbled Himself to Death

I was turkey hunting and killing kudzu at our river cabin in Georgia. It was midspring, the trees all decked out in their new foliage, forty degree mornings, eighty degree afternoons. Blue-bird skies, wild flowers blooming, turkeys gobbling, birds singing, everything fresh and new.

The Mitchell family came up to visit, and Matt my nephew, who loves the outdoors wanted to go turkey hunting. He's an avid deer and bird hunter but had never been turkey hunting in the spring.

The night before we were going hunting we ate fried wild turkey, rice, lima beans, squash casserole and strawberry shortcake. I like to eat a lot of wild game and fish. I believe I absorb a little of their power of the wild and that helps me catch or kill 'em. I ate an extra helping of that wild turkey that night. I told Matt to do the same, 'cause being fairly new to calling and yelping the birds, we needed all the help we could get.

Sunday morning was perfect. Bright stars in the sky, cool and still.

We walked to the top of the hill up from the cabin. It's one of the highest points of land in the county, standing two hundred feet above the Flint River with big hardwood trees growing thick all the way down. It was a grand place to hoot like an owl and listen for any birds gobbling back. You could hear 'em for miles.

I ask Matt if he could hoot like an owl. He said, "pretty good," so I told 'em to try it.

He hooted and a turkey gobbled back immediately.

"Can't hunt that one," I said, "he's across the river, hoot again".

Matt hoots and the same turkey answers back, and then another one gobbles down the river on our side.

Matt hoots one more time to give us a better fix on where the turkey is and the bird gobbles again, and then triple gobbles on top of that.

We take off, needing to get as close as we can before daylight.

Down these steep ravines we go, crunching through the dry leaves, snapping off unseen limbs in the thick places, stumbling in old rotted stump holes, holding on, sliding, trying not to roll down that hill.

The turkey keeps right on gobbling. He's hot to trot and waiting on daylight. It's every turkey hunter's dream, mine especially, 'cause I love to hear 'em gobble. Really love to have 'em answer me when I yelp at 'em. I'm hot to get setup and start talking to that bird.

We finally reached the bottom in one piece. It enters my mind for the tenth of a second that it's going to be tough, toting this big gobbler up that hill.

I'll just have to let Matt do it, he's younger.

We cross the creek and setup on a dim old log road that winds its way up the steep side of that ravine. The woods now are just a mass of black shadows with small amounts of blue-gray showing through the canopy of leaves, telling us sun-up's just minutes away.

We're as close as we can get. Our property ends and the bird's roosted on the other side of the steep hill in another ravine. We'll just have to call 'em to us. Easier said than done, but the bird sounds willing.

Well, as I said before, I love to hear turkeys gobble and I love to talk to 'em and have 'em answer. I must have been in heaven that morning cause this bird was the talkingest, gobblingest bird I've ever been around. He almost wore me out calling and yelping.

I'd yelp and he'd gobble and double gobble and triple gobble.

I'd refrain from yelping and he'd gobble at me to make me yelp. I'd yelp again and he'd cut me out, not even waiting for me to finish before he'd shake the leaves gobbling, catch his breath and gobble some more.

But he wasn't moving. He was screaming at me to come to him, as is the natural order of things, but that's something I could not do. Number one, he'd see me and do the haul-ass, number two, I didn't want to stray that far over on my neighbor's property.

The bird gobbled at least a hundred times, maybe more. I yelped back at him half that many times, til my lips got numb and the roof of my mouth got sore. I know, according to good turkey hunters, that you're not suppose to yelp near that much, but I couldn't help it. I had finally found a bird that loved to talk to me and I couldn't help but be sociable and respond in a polite manner by holding up my end of the conversation.

He wouldn't come. I could just picture what that bird was doing. He was excited, mad and horny. Strutting and gobbling, wanting to fight or make love, whoever showed up first. Too busy stating his case to bother trotting over to that poor-mouthed bird with the ugly voice, which was me.

I tried a trick to get 'em to come on so we could ease his pain and put some number six lead aspirins in his head. I love to hear 'em but I like to shoot 'em too if I can get 'em up to thirty or forty yards.

I waved Matt over to where I was and told him to sit tight and watch up that old dim road. I was sure that old gobbler would walk down it when he came. The light was good in the woods now as I crossed back over the creek, yelping as I went, trying to make that cocky gobbler think I was leaving, going away from 'em and make 'em chase after me.

He'd gobble his head off every time I'd yelp.

He moved.

We could tell by the direction and intensity of his gobbling that he'd moved north of where he'd been and he was close, just over the top of that ravine.

I'd yelp, he'd gobble, I'd yelp, he'd gobble. I'd stop yelping and he'd gobble, gobble, gobble, either challenging me or inviting me for love. I ain't deciphered their language yet, me a hundred yards from where I'd originally started calling from.

Then he quit.

The woods were quiet for a full ten minutes. Straining my eyes out looking for 'em. Knowing he was sneaking up to eyeball us but he never showed or at least we didn't see 'em.

Thirty minutes we waited after his last gobble. Me yelping and yelping trying to get a response, but no luck.

Another bird started gobbling at us from across the river, but he was satisfied being on that side and wouldn't come over.

Never have I heard such gobbling. For over an hour that bird gobbled non-stop. I'd have bet money we were going to kill that big ole gobbler.

I truly think that the reason we didn't get to see 'em or shoot 'em was, because he gobbled himself to death before he got there.

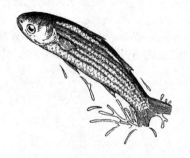

Poke Salad

We were sitting around the dinner table one night, up at the cabin in Georgia.

We'd just finished eating grilled pork chops, sweet potatoes, collard greens and pecan pie. All of us had a drink (we'd had a few), or a glass of wine and we were shooting the breeze about greens, collards and turnips, how we liked 'em cooked, if we liked the turnip roots, etc. Just friendly, relaxed conversation.

Buster, my good buddy who was born and raised in middle Georgia, asks us if we know what poke salad is.

We'd all heard of it, one of my favorite songs is "Poke Salad Annie". We knew it was a type of green that grew wild in the woods but nobody knew much about it.

Buster did.

Buster told us that his favorite thing to eat in the world is fresh turnip greens cooked with the roots, and homemade cornbread.

When he went off to college, he didn't get any home cooking during the week and looked forward to getting home on Friday afternoon and making up for all the meals he'd missed away at school.

Buster's family had a cook. I can't recall her name, Effie Mae, Earnestine or something like that, a real homegrown down to earth, southern country cook. A big black lady that knew what she was doing.

She knew Buster loved greens and cornbread and always tried to have some on the stove when Buster came home on Friday afternoons.

This particular Friday afternoon, Buster came home hungry, starving to death, looking forward to some home cooking.

He wasn't disappointed. There were two big pots of greens on the stove and warm cornbread in the oven.

Buster gets down a bowl to eat some greens in, and I don't mean he gets a cereal bowl or ice cream bowl. He got himself a real bowl, a bowl like you use to mix a cake in, a bowl like you use to serve the whole family in at the table.

He got 'em some cornbread, salt, pepper, some butter, plenty of pot liquor in the big bowl with his greens to sop the cornbread in, and chowed down.

Boy they were good, seasoned with fatback, and hot, he wolfed down a whole cake bowl full. He even got a second helping. Not the whole bowl full, just a little bit in the bottom of the bowl, about a quart to finish off his cornbread with.

Then Buster's thoughts turned to other things besides food.

He was home for the weekend from his freshman year of college. He had a brand new 440 Roadrunner in the circular driveway outside (this circular driveway plays a part later), a date to the dance with Mary Sue tonight, a date to the movies with Sally Jean Saturday night and an appointment with the boys down at the river at midnight to do a little drinking and hell raising.

He goes in and takes a shower, shaves, puts on deodorant and a half-a-pint of "Canoe", perfume for men. Got to smell good for the girls. New Gant shirt, stiff Levis, shiny boots, hair all slickered down. Ready to rock-n-roll and howl at the moon; let's get started.

Time to pick up Mary Sue.

Buster goes out the door, stepping high, full of anticipation for the coming night's events. Jumps in that new Roadrunner, fires her up, revving the engine just to hear it roar, puts it in gear, takes off out that circular driveway and learns about Poke Salad.

You see in Middle Georgia, at that time, the black folk of the area believed that they needed to "clean the system out", once or twice a year. Clean the system out of the whole family, children, grandparents, parents, aunts, uncles and cousins. To do that they all ate, and made everybody else in the family eat, a small helping of Poke Salad. Buster's cook lady had picked a mess for her family, cooked it up while she was cooking Buster's turnips, and had gone out to the store when Buster got home.

Buster had eaten most all of a pot of Poke Salad that was intended to "clean out" a family of about twenty people.

Back to Buster.

He goes out that circular drive, squealing his tires a little with those four hundred and forty cubic inches. Takes a hard right, takes another hard right back into the driveway on the other side, pulls up to the door and takes off to the bathroom. Fast walk this time, just some mild stomach cramps propelling him along.

No big deal. Does his business, heads out of the house, jumps back in the car, cranks it up and heads out again.

Thank God for that circular driveway.

If he'd had to turn the car around, instead of just going in a circle and pulling back in, he'd never made it.

Run this time into the house. Run all the way through the house and into the bathroom.

Buster didn't make his date with Mary Sue on Friday. Didn't make his date with Sally on Saturday night either. Didn't even think about meeting the boys at the river. He didn't leave the bathroom for the next two days. Buster made it back to college on Monday, weak as a kitten and ten pounds lighter.

Buster knows what Poke Salad is. Buster knows what Poke Salad does. Buster still loves greens, collards, turnips and roots, but he don't get 'em out of the pot unless the cook's around.

A Good Bass Fisherman

We have one of the prettiest places in the state of Georgia. It's in middle Georgia on the Flint River. The river roars like a big mountain stream where our place is. There's rock shoals and a three-foot drop in elevation in the river so the water's moving fast.

I was standing on one of those big rocks in the middle of the river catching red bellies for my supper. I was alone, nobody for miles, intent on putting my cricket in a little eddy where the bream like to lay. Out of the corner of my eye I caught some movement. The movement I'd seen was a small shoal bass, about ten inches long, flopping up and down, back and forth on the edge of a small sandbar sticking outta the water.

The reason he was flopping around on the edge of that sandbar was because a nice fat snake had 'em by the nose.

The snake couldn't handle that bass in the water, so he was dragging 'em out.

The bass would flop back and forth, back and forth in the shallows. Every time he'd flop he'd jerk the snake's head back and forth with 'em.

The snake just held on, steady backing up on the sand with a sort of sideways crawl, inching that bass up on dry land. Holding his nose like a bulldog.

Every flop the fish would make the snake would drag 'em higher on the sand til the bass was clear out of the water.

When the fish was completely out of the water, he really went frantic with his jumping and thrashing, some times lifting ten inches of the snake off the ground.

But the snake held on. Just laying there now that the fish was clear, waiting for the bass to give up, knowing somehow that a fish outta water calms right down sooner or later.

Flop, long pause. Another feeble flitter by the fish. A real long pause. A couple of little twitches and the fish lays still.

I've never though about it before, but now that I've seen it happen, bass, especially small bass, are shaped just right to slide nicely down a hungry fat snake's throat.

I'd check the progress between bream bites, on how ole fat-boy was coming with his dinner and once the fish stopped moving, it didn't take five minutes before the snake was laying on the sandbar by himself with a nice fat lump in his belly.

I've got to get me a book on snakes. These Georgia snakes are a lot different than Florida snakes. I'd never seen a pink snake before. A pink snake, about three feet long, big bodied with red looking strips going around his body. Clay, my youngest son, told me he'd seen a pink snake swim across the river and I didn't know if I believed 'em or not til now.

I can tell you this, those pink Georgia river snakes are damned good bass fishermen. I think the limit's one bass per snake, per day, cause he couldn't hold another one in his belly and I didn't see a stringer.

Georgia Redneck Sunday Afternoon

We have the greatest neighbors you could have at our place in Taylor County, Georgia. They own the hundred acre tract next door and live on it, maintaining a beautiful home and yard, in a small pecan grove surrounded by planted pines. Both our places border the Flint River, they're beautiful and remote.

If you love to hunt and fish you're in heaven. Other than that, there's not much to do. Town's a long way off and nothing's going on there anyway.

My neighbors are outdoors people. Man, wife, two grown sons. They hunt, fish, grow fruits and vegetables, work fifty hour weeks for big companies in Macon. They eat wild game and fresh bream and catfish all year long. They eat a lot of good wild pork too cause they also hunt and trap the wild hogs that are so destructive to their fields and gardens.

I was passing by their place about noon. I'd been scouting for turkey sign for the coming season, was going home for lunch.

One the boys waved me in the yard, I could see they had a hog strung up, skinning 'em out.

As I pulled up, I could hear more hogs grunting and squealing in the back of Troy's truck. They had trapped five that morning.

"How about some fresh pork?" he asks, "We got plenty of it."

"I see you do," I said as I got out and looked in the back of the pickup. It's half full of tied-up, wild eyed, grunting wild hogs.

Pretty things, round and fat and shiny and black from all the corn, peanuts, soybeans and peaches they've been chowing down on, outta the farmer's fields.

"Take one with you," Troy says as he finishes cutting loose all the hog's insides, that fall intact into a number two washtub that's essential to every household of the south.

"I'll damn sure do it," I say as I look at that inch of pure white fat covering that pig, take in those pretty pink hams and shoulders, those ribs on the grill, that tenderloin in the frying pan.

Troy works the now dressed pig loose from the gimbling stick, stuck through his hind legs as I hold the pig up, and we throw 'em in a big ice chest in the back of my truck.

"We're getting ready to do the rest of 'em," Troy says as he drags another hog out the back of his truck.

"Can you believe we caught five of 'em this morning?" "That one you got we had to shoot, he couldn't get in the pen it was so full, but he hung around the others on the outside long enough for us to kill 'em."

I notice Chad, Troy's younger brother come out of the house with Princess, their mama's pet bulldog and tie her to a post.

Princess is whining and barking and wiggling and squirming all around, like bulldogs do when they're excited. She smelled and saw and heard those tied up hogs, wanting to get at 'em.

Troy starts toting and dragging the pig he's got out of the truck, out into his mama's perfectly manicured yard and pecan grove. Around the flower beds, past the neat vegetable garden he goes, stopping about fifty yards from where Princess is tied.

Troy kneels down getting ready to cut the ropes off the now squealing and jumping hog.

Chad's ready with the video cam and set to turn "Princess" loose when Troy gives the word.

Mr. Ben, the boy's daddy yells, "Don't let that damn hog get away to ruin our fields again."

"Don't worry, Pop," shouts Troy as he cuts loose the hog, "I've hamstrung 'em a little bit so he can't run too fast."

The hog squeals and runs. Chad turns the dog loose.

"Princess" takes off after 'em, sorta squealing herself with excitement.

Chad's right behind her, camera rolling to record the chase and the catch.

Princess does her job catching the squealing hog by the nose and laying down and bringing the hog with her.

"Good Princess," "Good Princess" the boys yell as they straddle both hog and dog, trying to get Princess to turn loose. They finally get the dog off, pull out a .22 pistol, shoot the hog between the eyes, drag 'em back to the game cleaning area and string 'em up on the hoist.

As I'm driving off to leave with my fresh pork all iced down in the cooler, I see Chad, tying Princess back to her post, Troy dragging another trussed up hog out of the truck and through the yard.

They're fixing to lift the curtain on Scene Two of a Georgia Redneck Sunday afternoon.

What is it about fish?

What is it about fish?

How can they wield so much power over people. Men and women. How do they do it?

They must have special hypnotic powers that they've used on everybody that's ever caught one, or anybody that's even watched one being caught.

The spell that they cast is so powerful that it can even be absorbed by people looking at fish in photographs.

Sometimes I think the photograph spells they cast is even more powerful than when you're exposed to the live fish itself.

It don't matter the type or specie of the fish. Little bream dangling from a line on a homemade cane pole fishing from a ditch bank seem to have the same power on a person as gazing in the eyes of a thousand pound Blue Fin Tuna attached to a steel leader, connected to a two thousand dollar rod and reel, fished from the deck of a half million dollar charter rig.

People freeze in the winter trying to catch 'em, burn up in the summer. They're late for work, take off early from work, even loose their jobs, all in the name of trying to get a critter that lives in the water, out of it.

There's one other fish habit, that one's susceptible to, that's even worse than just catching fish.

That's catching fish and selling 'em for money.

Don't ever do it.

Don't ever even give your neighbor a mess of fish and let 'em give you two dollars towards gas or bait.

You'll be ruined.

If you ever go fishing and catch fish and turn 'em into hundreds or even thousands of dollars, you've had it. You're whole life will be changed. You'll spend the rest of your life and all the money you can get your hands on, trying to catch fish, and more fish and even more fish!

If you're lucky, you'll go broke quick and be forced, at an early age, to revert back to more traditional, eight to five ways to make a living.

I just don't know how to tell you to keep from getting this infectious disease called fishing.

Ya need to eat 'em.

They're good for you, the vitamin and minerals and such.

I guess canned fish would be safe, sardines, tuna fish.

I'm thinking that if you even look at 'em too long, iced-down in a showcase in the fish market, they'll throw that hypnotic power on you.

Be careful.

I think it would be a good point to debate as to who hooks who in this deal we call fishing.

BIG TROUT   CLAY MARSHALL LOVEL   6- -99

Big Trout

We caught two big, big trout last trip out.

Big for our area anyway.

One weighed seven pounds.

The other six.

Another thing that made the fish extraordinary was what they had in 'em.

Ben and Clay both remarked, when they tripped 'em in the boat with the mullet, "You got to come look at this".

What I saw when I got there was two huge trout with full grown mullet tails sticking out the sides of their mouths.

When you picked the fish up with both hands you could feel the head and body of the mullet in the trout's body and see his tail sticking out his mouth.

Amazing.

Looked like the poor old trout would gag.

I would, trying to eat something that big.

I wonder if that's the reason they don't catch many really big trout on hook and line cause they don't use big enough bait.

Ever see anybody fishing for trout with a one pound, twelve inch mullet hooked on his line for bait?

Cause that's what those mullet weighed when we pulled 'em outta the trout back at the fish house.

Now, did those trout weight 6 and 7 pounds; or did they weigh 5 and 6 pounds?

Do you count the mullet or not?

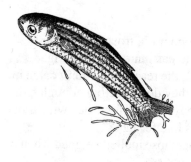

They Had Rather Catch People

Some Marine Patrol Officers really love their job.

I think some Marine Patrol officers love to catch people better than people love to catch fish!

I watched an ole master at people- catching at work a few years ago.

We were grading rock bass down at the fish house and Joel, the local Marine Patrol officer, walked up.

Now we'd all known Joel for years and dealt with him many times. He'd always worn the bruise colored uniform of the Florida Marine Patrol, black and gray, but this day was different.

This day he had on blue jeans, an old faded plaid shirt, a baseball cap and something I'd never seen, a can of Budweiser in his hand.

"Joel, I never knew you drank."

"Don't," he says. "Picked this can up outta the garbage right there," he points, turning the can upside down to show it was empty.

"What are you doing?" I say.

"Waiting on somebody," he replies and then starts commenting on the rock bass we're grading to change the subject.

Right then I took a quick inventory of the boats in the marina. I thought they were all in, then I noticed Barney's boat was out.

Barney's one the best hook and line trout fishermen I've ever known. Trout are his passion and he's damn good at catching 'em. He lives in Atlanta and almost always fishes til dark. He's been known, from time to time, to catch his limit, bring 'em in and go catch another limit; sometimes maybe a few over the limit.

It had to be Barney that Joel was waiting for.

Just as the sky is getting all pinky red, I see Barney's boat idling up our canal.

He ties up to the floating dock, gets out, grabs a beer from his cooler and starts to chat with the other fishermen who'd been out that day.

Ten minutes pass, Joel stays over here with us.

Fifteen minutes go by, Joel's paying no attention to anyone and I wonder what's going on.

Finally I ask Joel.

"That's the last boat in."

I know it's Barney he's waiting for and it's 7 p.m., way past Joel's suppertimes.

"What ya waiting for?" I ask.

"I'm waiting for 'em to get the rest of his fish," Joel says and goes back to watching us grade rock bass.

Barney visits with Hubert and Dirk. No hurry, he's home on safe ground, it's dark and everything is just fine. It's been a good day and he's happy.

There's no way to warn Barney with Joel standing right beside me, wish I could have.

Sure enough, Barney gets his ice chest out of his boat, carries it to the fish cleaning table and dumps it out. A nice catch of beautiful silver gold speckled trout, laying on the table, glistening in the overhead lights, some still flopping and gasping around.

Then Barney disappears in the shadows behind the marina building and comes back straining, carrying another ice chest and dumps it on the table with the other fish.

"That's what I'm waiting for," Joel says as he pitches his empty "disguising" beer can back in the garbage can he got it from.

Marching over to where Barney is in a half walk, half run, he fishes his badge out of his pocket and shows it to Barney.

Barney looks at his nice catch and shrugs.

Joel looks at his nice catch and smiles.

My Wife and the Bay

If I could only pick two things to credit for getting me through this life, I'd have to first pick my wife, Mary Jane, and then the bay. If I could pick more than two I'd add my sons, parents, a few friends and family members, Dog Island and Georgia, the state of, middle Georgia to be exact, but since there can only be two, it's Mary Jane and the bay.

I love Mary Jane more than the bay (she'll argue this point), and I finally figured out, I love them both for a lot of the same reasons.

Both hold much power over me, the power to make me very happy or extremely sad or mad. I can't resist 'em when they call, my mind is on one or the other all the time or both at the same time.

Their beauty and strength intrigue me, never tiring of looking at either one, seeing more beauty, depth and mystery the harder I look, and the longer I know 'em.

Their shared ability of motherhood, link them. Mary Jane producing sons and families, the bay the mother of millions of types of life.

There are many differences in the two main loves of my life.

The bay is uncaring and unforgiving, it doesn't matter to the bay your feelings, your mistakes. Those mistakes possibly helping the bay if it's a serious one, making more food for the fishes and crabs, the bay's children. The bay won't come and stand beside you when times are tough, like Mary Jane will, or comfort you when you're down and out. The bay is likely to kick you when you're down, with a storm or hurricane or bad fishing year. It's not that it's mean or hateful, it's just the bay, uncaring, unforgiving, wild.

The bay scares me sometimes. My wife never would. I fear for her sometimes but I don't fear her, she wouldn't want me to.

They both can be stormy at times. It's best just to hunker down and ride it out, throw out the anchor and stay put. Doing and saying little or nothing is most times safest. Waiting for the storm to pass and the sun to come back out in a smile.

They both can be full of surprises and change moods without warning.

They're both so resilient and tough when it comes to crisis and adversity.

They're wonders, is what they are. Miracles of life and I'm proud to be associated to and seen with them.

I hope I never have to pick between one or the other, but if I did it would be without hesitation, I'd pick Mary Jane. My wife, my partner, my friend, my heart, for without her I wouldn't have the strength and drive to face the other, nor the will to carry on.

They can both hurt you, one just mentally, the bay both mentally and physically. Neither one really meaning to, it just happens.

Maybe I hurt them and they're just paying me back. I don't mean to, I'm just a human being, stupid sometimes; thoughtless; but not often.

I respect 'em, love 'em both, hope to spend to the rest of my life with 'em. I pray one of 'em doesn't get jealous and kill me, the uncaring, unforgiving one.

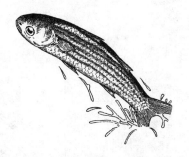

FISHING IN THE NIGHT FOG   CLAY MARSHALL LOVEL   7- -99

Fishing in the Night Fog

We love to mullet fish.

Before the gill net ban in '95 we fished day and night for run mullet, mullet with red roe. It was an important part of our livelihood.

This particular night it was foggy and still but the sky was clear and you had plenty of milky moonlight to see by. Everything was shadows and mists and water. If you make the mistake of turning on a spotlight, the fog would throw the light back at you and make you blind for a few minutes. As long as you didn't turn it on you could do all right.

Ben and I were easing up Walker Creek at idle in my old wooden mullet skiff, listening and looking for the fish to whirl up in the water.

We didn't have to look far. The fish weren't bunched up, but every bend in every creek showed fish sign.

We'd pitch out the staff and strike, two to three hundred yards of the six hundred yards we had, of monofilament gill net, cut the motor off and listen to the fish hit the net.

I've fished these creeks for twenty years, mostly in the daytime. Nighttime on the water is always a new experience, even if you've been where you are a thousand times. Nights like this night was, is really a trip.

It's totally still and quiet. In late November there are no night sounds like birds, insects or frogs.

There's no horizon.

There's no up, seems to be no down.

The marsh grass looks like solid black walls where it meets the water of the creek and the water looks like thick black oil only disturbed by the movement of your boat and the whirling splashing of the fish as they fight the net.

We take the net up with no light.

The moon makes the mullet shine like little silver colored missiles as they dangle in the invisible webbing. You shuck 'em through the net by feel, long ago losing the need to look at 'em to do it, even in the daytime.

You don't talk much, if we do, it's in a quiet whisper, not wanting to break the spell of the night, the silence, the darkness, the peace.

Clear the net.

Find more fish.

Strike it off again.

Each time you strike and shut the motor off, the silence, combined with the fog almost puts a weight on your body. You feel the need to hold on to something when you move from place to place on the boat, your sense of balance challenged by the dark and quiet. You're glad to have the weight of the net in your hands. Something to hold onto, stabilize yourself with, something to concentrate on.

When the net's cleared, the box is full. Six, seven hundred pounds of Mother Nature's finest. Time to head back to Spring Creek and unload.

As you plane the boat off, eyes now fully adjusted to the dark you get the sensation that the world's moving by you. That you're not moving at all. There's no vibration from wavelets on the water cause it's slick calm. There's no white wake trailing out behind the boat cause the fog swallows it up. It's just you, motionless. Watching the eerie shadow shrouded world being paraded by you until your destination comes by and you stop the world from moving and get out of the boat.

Back to hard ground.

Back to electric lights.

Back to sounds.

Back to earth from a trip in space.

Spring Gobbler Opening Week March '99 or The "Tour de Kill"

Charlie Thomas

Let me begin with Charlie Thomas, one of our best friends and turkey hunting mentor.

Somewhere in Charlie's ancestry, way down the line, past great-great grandfathers, there must have been a very lonely ancestor. This ancestor must have only had a turkey hen for a companion. What I'm trying to say is that Charlie Thomas has turkey genes.

He's got to.

Nobody could talk turkey like he does but even more important, think turkey like he does, unless he had turkey blood in 'em somewhere down the line.

Charlie knows what the birds are saying.

Charlie knows what he's saying back.

He knows whether the turkey's lonely, and calls back sweetly.

He knows when the turkey's horny and calls back sexily.

He knows when the bird is mad and challenging, and challenges 'em to come and fight.

By looking at a track he knows the sex of the bird, where they're going, where they've been and how far they're going to travel.

He's one of the best woodsmen and fishermen I've ever known and he's been gracious enough with me and my sons to share some of his knowledge.

All these turkey stories I hope to write are in some way connected to his shared knowledge even though, I'm proud to say, we're finally learning enough to hunt, call and kill some gobblers on our own.

Thanks, Charlie Thomas!

On Our Own

Monday afternoon Charlie, Ben and Jason had found some turkey sign on Homer's property north of Butler, Georgia.

We call it the Powerline, for obvious reasons, or Turkey Valley depending on what part of the property we're on.

What you've got is a big, deep, wet, hardwood filled ravine with clear-

201

cuts on either side, a power line running through the clear-cuts with planted pines bordering the whole thing.

The birds love it in the spring.

We parked in the planted pines about 5:15 on Tuesday morning, and eased out, lightly closing the doors on the trucks, to listen for gobblers.

The sky was just starting to show a break in the blue-black night on the horizon to the east when the coyotes must have caught something down in the bottom land. The hell they raised with their howling and yipping made the hair stand up on your neck and reminded you that there still is a primitive, wild, survival of the fittest world out there as much as we seem to forget it.

No turkeys gobbling anywhere.

Since the coyotes quit their howling the woods have been quiet and we could have heard most anything being up high like we were on top of that hill.

Charlie and Jason decide to go west, me and Ben go down the hill and east, knowing there's turkey in the area but not where.

The sky's graying up and the temperature starts to drop as it seems to do right at daybreak. We need to set up somewhere, but where?

East we go, fixing to set up on the edge of the clear-cut and some eight year old pines, when we spy a set of large gobbler tracks, made the evening before, in the stark white sand of the road we're on.

They're going in the opposite direction of where we're headed.

We stop.

What to do, which way to go?

Go the way the tracks do, walk into the pines before the sun gets up. Follow your instinct and go where you think the birds would go.

Try to think like a turkey.

Ben and I had never called one on our own. We were learning to yelp and cluck, put and purr. We'd tried to call turkeys but had never been successful.

We were fixing to try again.

Out of the clear cut we went, easing quiet through some ten-foot pines to the head of a small bottom, thick with briars, brush and small hardwoods.

Ben and I split up, one to set up on either side of the branch, back in the small pines, knowing where each other would be, about fifty yards apart.

We agreed we would both yelp as we saw fit and see what happened. We still hadn't heard any birds but it was time to get still, quiet and hide. The sun was starting to break the horizon and we sure didn't want to be seen by the birds before they flew down from the roost.

I made my own little nest under a bushy pine in the briars as the sun came up, making the light frost all twinkley in the light and your breath thick and smokey in front of your face.

The cardinals make their first peeping calls of the morning.

The wrens start to flutter and flit from bush to bush, waking up and hunting each other. It's getting light enough to see good.

I yelp real soft.

I hear Ben yelp.

Silence, five minutes goes by, Ben yelps again, so do I a few seconds later. Maybe we'll sound inviting to somebody.

The sun's well over the horizon now, the heat bringing a light misty fog off the ground, making everything gray-white except for the bright green of the tops of the pines as they catch the direct sunlight.

The woods come alive.

Squirrels bark in the bottoms, jays squawk, cardinals chirp, wood ducks call and you can hear their wings whistle as they fly over head.

Way far in the distance, to the north and west, you faintly hear a raspy soft sound that you know is a gobbler a long way off, sitting on the roost and announcing to the world that it's spring and that he's king of his territory and that it's time to propagate the specie, that I don't drink and I don't eat this time of the year, that I gobble, fight and make love, that I've only got three months out of the twelve to do this in and here I am, come and get it, which ever one you want, fighting or loving, I'm ready.

I hear 'em again and know Ben must hear 'em too.

I have to turn around 180 degrees from where I'm facing to be ready if he comes.

I yelp, Ben yelps, the turkey gobbles again.

A faint "poof" of a sound. A sound we know to be a shotgun in the distance.

Wonder who that was? Was it Charlie and Jason? Could they have killed one already? It's only 6:30.

The turkey gobbles again, still far away, can't tell if he's coming yet.

Then another turkey gobbles, and I mean he really gobbles and he gobbles loud and clear and long from now directly behind us, in the original direction we were facing.

I yelp, Ben yelps.

Gobble, gobble, gobble, gobble, the turkey answers.

I turn around again to face the other way, this bird much closer than the other one!

The turkey gobbles again, louder it seems.

I think he's coming this way, can't be positive yet but I think he is.

He gobbles again.

He's definitely coming closer

I yelp, Ben yelps.

The turkey answers and he is coming fast.

We stay quiet, no yelping from either one of us.

Gobble, gobble, gobble, gobble, he's coming around Ben's side of the branch

Ben, quiet as he should be, not calling.

Gobble, gobble, gobble, gobble

You can't describe it when you know that bird's right here with you, heart beating in your ears, everything in the world forgotten as that basic instinct takes over, you trying to pluck one of nature's finest creatures from its home habitat. Trying to see an animal with ten times the eyesight perception that we have, before he sees you. Knowing that if you do see 'em before he sees you that he'll be in shotgun range and you'll have one-half of one eye blink to aim and fire at that blood red or ice-white head. That you won't get a second chance.

Gobble, gobble, gobble, gobble.

So loud the leaves seem to shake on the trees. The only sound now in the woods is the gobbling sound, at least the only sound you're tuned to, so close that you know something is fixing to happen, either a shot, the alarmed "put" of the turkey as he spies you or the great beating of wings or running of feet as the bird makes his escape.

The bird gobbles, again, closer, so close, but you can't see 'em, he hasn't moved since he gobbled last, wary, suspicious, wanting you to come to him, as is the natural order of things with the hens.

Softly, lightly, I cluck three times.

Silence, no reply.

Silence, the sun's well up, the pine woods are bright with light.

BAM, pause, BAM again.

Flop, flop, flop, flop

Ya Hoooooooooooooooooo, I hear as I jump up, checking the sky as I do in case the bird has flown my way.

Ya Hoooooooooooooooooo. Weeeeeeeeeeeeeeeee, Ben yells as I pick up speed heading through the frosty woods towards Ben.

What a sight, my oldest son Ben, 12 ga. double barrel in his left hand, big, still flopping gobbler in his right hand, by the neck, running through the pines leaping and hollering like an Indian, looking for me with his first big gobbler.

Damn, what a war dance we did.

Dancing, high-fiving, hugging, tearing off our face masks, looking at the turkey's head, admiring his fighting spurs, awed at the colors of his feathers, guessing his weight, howling, whooping, primitive in our actions for the moment, almost over whelmed by the glory of the moment, proud of our accomplishments together.

Quickly and strangely we become quiet again, whispering to each other, reliving the hunt, the calls, the excitement, the gobbling of the bird, his approach, Ben's shot.

We whisper in wonder at this magnificent bird nature's been so kind to give us, feeling his spurs, and patting his feathers down smooth, studying his feet and beard, marveling at his ice blue head and blood red wattle.

Heartbeat down near normal, we gather up our gear.

Ben proudly reaches down and picks up his bird, by his feet and slings him over his shoulder, his wings coming half way open as he hangs down over Ben's back, the sunlight catching all the colors of the bird's breast feathers, the iridescent browns and greens changing colors from the different angles of the sunlight.

We walk casually back through the woods, back to the truck, the need for steath and silence now over, to brag and strut ourselves to Charlie and Jason about what good hunters we are. We hope that Jason could have the good luck to bag a bird himself, it would be his first, to make it a perfect morning if it could be any more perfect.

Guess what, that "poof" we heard in the distance right at daylight was Jason's shot. Him and Charlie had spied a gobbler walking down the road just at gray day. Charlie clucked one time, the turkey stopped and gobbled back, then making a beeline through the pines to the sound.

Jason got his bird, one shot.

Ben's got his bird.

The morning <u>was</u> absolutely perfect.

No Turkeys in the Area

It's Wednesday morning, another clear beautiful morning, a little warmer than the day before.

Jason and Ben had gone home Tuesday evening. Charlie and I were going to turkey hunt all week and we'd come back to the power line to try that area again.

I headed further east from where Ben and I had hunted the day before, Charlie telling me that we'd scared all the birds off from that area we hunted Tuesday with our whooping and war dance we'd done after Ben killed his bird. I take to heart all the advice Charlie gives when it comes to turkey hunting.

I found my spot before daylight, got settled in and looked for my callers.

Couldn't find 'em.

Couldn't believe it. All this way from the truck and I've got everything but what I need the most, my callers.

I walk back, searching the road in the half-dark, thinking maybe I'd dropped 'em getting out my gloves.

No luck, I find 'em on the seat of the truck where I'd left 'em.

Charlie is nowhere around, so I decide to go down in Turkey Valley and check it out.

I walk the whole ravine looking for tracks, scratchings or sign and find nothing but places the turkey's had used many days before, no tracks, nothing since the rain on Sunday night.

I never heard a bird gobble all morning, no clucks, yelps or anything and I had stopped and yelped in a bunch of different spots.

I walked the whole ravine. Crossed it, went back across it on the west end, searched the clear cut, crossed the power line into the planted pines, walked and yelped them out, and at nine thirty made my way back to the truck.

Charlie had been there since eight, waiting on me with a nice gobbler he'd killed at seven. A bird only Charlie Thomas would and could have killed.

He'd heard the bird gobble with his "ears", an electric assisted hearing device that allows 'em to listen for birds at great distances.

The bird was about two miles away, (he showed me later that morning) said he simply walked the two miles, listening to the bird as he went, til he got close enough to set up. He yelped once, the bird came, he shot 'em, walked the two miles back.

Nice bird too, 17-18 pounds, six-inch beard, one-inch spurs.

I'd seen or heard nothing, was going to tell Charlie there were no birds in the area, but I decided not to. Didn't want to make a fool of myself seeing as he had managed to find and kill a nice one. Told him I didn't see "much."

We loaded up in the truck and headed for Greenville, Alabama to hunt turkeys on Mr. Bates farm that afternoon, and that's my next story.

Alabama Birds

We'd been invited to hunt on Mr. Bates farm outside of Greenville, Alabama, close to a place called Fort Deposit.

Beautiful farm Mr. Bates has, his grandfather's homestead house is still standing, built in 1863. The house sets on the same place that Mr. Bates' great-grandfather built on in 1829. The farm itself is about 600 acres of rolling hills with hardwood bottoms, ponds and pastures, pecan groves and pine trees. Perfect turkey grounds for spring gobblers. Matter of fact, we saw one strutting gobbler when Mr. Bates was driving us around, showing us the farm.

About four o'clock Charlie and I drove back to the area we'd spotted that strutting turkey in and Charlie told me to go hunt that turkey and he'd look around for some more birds.

I got my gun and my gear and slipped along the edge of the hardwoods and set up on a steep slope with pines and hardwoods mixed. A small pond was up above me and a pasture was seventy to eighty yards below me.

I know the turkeys are close, so I yelped real soft to begin with and got no reply.

I yelped louder.

Nothing.

I yelped again and hear three little clucks in reply but could see nothing.

Looking down into the pasture I saw a sight that makes any turkey hunter's heart jump. A big gobbler in full strut twirling in a slow circle, putting on a show.

He slowly starts heading away from me, walking two feet, full strut, twirl in a slow circle, walk two feet, strut again.

One hen appears, then another and then another, pecking and rambling as hen turkeys do. Paying no attention to my calling or the strutting gobbler, but staying in the same general areas as the male turkey.

Strutting and drumming the ole tom turkey heads away from me, at his slow, show-off pace, me yelping and clucking trying to get 'em to come my way but it's like he and the hens are deaf. They pay no attention, make no reply to any calls at all.

The tom starts to strut back in my direction, still on the edge of the pasture, not coming up the hill towards me but at least he's not headed away.

Have you ever heard a big gobbler drum when he's strutting?

I hadn't, but I sure have now cause for two hours that bird strutted and drummed on the edge of that pasture, his tail all fanned out, mooning me it seemed every time I yelped. I finally figured out he was showing me his best side when he did like that, twirling in that slow circle, trying to lure me down there to 'em.

And the noise that turkey makes when he drums is crazy. If you ever hear one you'll know why they call it drumming. There's a distinct "bump" when he fans all his feathers out and if you're close enough you can hear a light, short, humming sound that's hard to describe on paper. They say the sound's created when the bird fills with air to make his feathers stand up.

Strut and drum, strut and drum, hen's pecking about non-stop. Strut/

drum, strut/drum, I yelp every ten to fifteen minutes just to let that gobbler know I'm still there.

The hens start pecking their way up the hill toward me.

The gobbler's still in the pasture doing his thing.

I'm trying to keep up with all three hens, so one won't get too close to me, and make me out and give the whole show away.

The sun's getting low in the sky.

The hens are still feeding but I can't see but two of 'em.

The gobbler's in the pasture. I'm looking for that third hen, where is she?

I look back down in the pasture and the gobbler's gone, vanished like he's never been there.

Where is he?

For two hours he's been fifty yards away, strutting and having a big time, now he's gone. I can't yelp or cluck cause the hens are too close and they'll make me out and send alarm.

Where's that gobbler?

A half-minute has passed and I can't see 'em anywhere. I wonder if that third hen has slipped around behind me? I know the gobbler has got to still be down the hill from me somewhere.

Wrong.

I look hard, way over my left shoulder, and there he is, twenty feet away, red head and neck, long hairy beard sticking out, and that black hard eye taking me in.

When that old gobbler finally decided to check out all that yelping and clucking that had been coming all evening from up the hill, he didn't waste any time. He circled around a little bit and snuck up behind me to see who I was.

Instinct again, his and mine.

All I can do is roll over on my belly from a sitting position against that tree, snap my old twelve ga. to my shoulder and fire.

The old tom had his neck stretched out, his feet bunched under 'em, ready to make the haul-ass, but he was too slow that day, my number sixes found his head and neck and he was mine.

I was proud of that shot, as quick as I'd had to react but felt like a fool two seconds later when I jumped up to go get 'em and almost rolled down the hill on top of 'em. My feet had gone to sleep again during the long wait and when I jumped up everything moved but my feet, my body going down the hill and my legs staying up the hill putting me on my face and my gun barrel in the mud.

I learned three things that day: one, just cause the turkeys don't answer your calls doesn't mean they're not listening and remembering where you are; two, listen for that drumming sound, it'll tell you they're there when they won't call back; and three, get up slow after a long sit or you'll hurt yourself.

Flint River Sandbar Turkeys

The Bell family has a nine hundred acre farm that borders the Flint River for almost 2 miles.

We'd been invited to turkey hunt on the place one March morning with Glenn, one of the in-laws of the family. Glenn wanted to hunt with Charlie to gain a few pointers, so I hunted by myself.

Glenn gave me directions on what roads to follow that would wind me up at the river and I started out. Clear morning with stars and a half moon to light my way, following a dirt road that was going through fresh plowed fields and heading towards a black wall of gum and hardwood trees that made up the swamp that bordered the river.

It got darker and wetter as I walked into the hardwoods, the road winding, and twisting through the trees. The puddles and low places that held water showing the stars shining in 'em as the trees hadn't gotten their leaves back yet to block 'em out. Old broken down deer stands appeared in the gloom, built in big hickory trees on curves in the road.

Newer, metal ladder stands leaned against gum trees in different places, empty now with deer season being closed. Finally the road curved to the east, rose over a hump that's that bank of the river, and ended at a big sandbar on the west bank of the Flint.

The sand bar was about 200 yards long, and as I found out later, was too wide to shoot a turkey across. There wasn't one bit of cover on that sandbar, it was white and pretty in the starlight and clean as a whistle. On the high hump of the bank there was an old fallen tree laid right down in a briar patch with a lot of dead brush standing up in front of it.

That's where I set up, sitting on that dead tree, looking up and down the river through the bushes, listening for the first gobble of the morning.

I was facing east, looking at another black wall of hardwoods a hundred yard across the river, the sky just starting to show pink-orange, defining some of the big limbs on the trees across the way. Fish struck in the water, owls hooted, coyotes howled, wood ducks flew both ways, up and down the river, going to feed. Two of the woodies lit in the water in front of the sandbar, walked out and started to pick and preen their feathers, waiting on the sun.

A turkey gobbles up river from me.

Lord what that first gobble of the morning does to a man. Makes his ears try to grow bigger, makes his heart race, freezes all body motion and focuses his minds on one thing and one thing only.

Another turkey gobbles halfway from me to the first one, and then one gobbles straight across the river from me and he's got to be roosted right on the bank.

He gobbles again, and again and again, non-stop.

The sky's getting brighter now, most the eastern horizon orange in the glow of the coming sunrise.

I can see most all the branches on the bare trees across the river, looking hard for that turkey that gobbles constantly.

There he is.

He's in a big white oak tree about thirty feet off the ground, on a big dead limb that slopes in a slight angle up from the trunk of the tree.

He's in full strut on that limb, walking from one end to the other, gobbling, blowing up into a full strut, turning around walking to the end of the limb in the other direction, gobbling and doing it again.

I hear hens cluck in the trees.

I hear jakes try to gobble, making more like coughing sounds than gobbles.

Occasionally, there's another turkey that gobbles, but the big boss gobbling across the river breaks in every time they try, and besides that he doesn't give 'em a chance to gobble cause he never stops doing it, only long enough to walk from one end of that eight foot limb to the other.

The mist starts rising off the river, only five or six feet high, making it look like a long flowing cup of hot, black coffee, helping hide me across it on the other side.

I yelp real soft.

The turkey answers.

I yelp real soft again.

The turkey gobbles and gobbles, and gobbles, non stop again and then jumps off his limb and without flapping his wings, sails across the river and lands on the sandbar, gobbling the instant his feet hit the ground, then going into a full strut.

Slowly, so slowly he walks my way. Never leaving the edge of the river. Gobbling every five feet, but coming, slow.

He's seventy five yards down stream and seventy-five yards out from me, it's still gray-dark and yet I can see that long thick beard shaking every time he gobbles. I can make out his ice-white head and clearly see his big tail feathers when he fans it out.

Damn, I want to shoot 'em but he's just too far. I'll just have to wait for 'em to come a little closer.

Look at that bird gobble. He looks mean and ugly with his neck stretched out, parallel to the ground, feathers standing up like hair on a dog's back when he's fixing to bite you. Mouth wide open, unearthly sound coming out, feet throwing sand like a bull. Then he's calm, standing regally, at alert, looking.

Then he flies, he just jumps up and with a half a dozen, whump, whump, whumps of his great wings, flies back across the river and lights in a snag.

He never makes another sound.

I yelp.

No answer.

I yelp again.

Nothing.

The mist off the river turns to a pretty thick fog as the sun breaks the horizon and I can't even see 'em anymore. All the other turkeys have shut up and I guess I've blown my chance.

I'm not leaving. I'm not going anywhere.

That huge gobbler's just across the river and maybe I can call 'em back.

The sun clears the trees, making the sandbar yellow-white and the river sparkles and gurgles. Beautiful bright morning.

I have to come down off my perch on that dead tree cause the sun's shining right on me, making me feel like a Christmas tree bulb so I've got to hide better. I just slide down in the briars, lay over on my belly and ease up to the edge of the bank, peering through the briars, clucking and yelping every once in a while.

An hour goes by. No answers to my calls, no activity.

Wrens and sparrows flit all around me in the bushes, the sun's warm on my back and for once I'm not all cramped up from sitting in one position so long.

A turkey hen sails across the river and lights on the sandbar dead in front of me.

I know something's fixing to happen.

Two at one time come across, then three, then one. The turkeys are pouring across the river to that bar. Then I hear a totally different flying sound from the hens soft floating glide, the sound of lots of air being pumped as gobblers lift their bulk up from the other side of the river to join those hens on this side.

I'm almost scared to look at the birds through the bushes, they're so many turkey eyes over there to see me, but I peek as best I can without being seen and see two big gobblers come across, then a third.

I don't know how many turkeys are on that sandbar, but there's a bunch. Eighteen to twenty five and I know that there's at least three grown gobblers with 'em.

211

I'm going to get my second chance.

Calling's no good, there's too many birds together and one of the hens may come over here and make me.

They seem real content right now, one gobbler strutting, what hens I can see seem to be just warming up in the sun, but I can't see real good cause I can't raise my head up or move at all without being seen.

I glimpse one big gobbler off to the side of the main pack of birds. The sun's shining bright now, showing off all his colors and I can't take my eyes off that big beard hanging down like a paint brush off his chest.

I think he's in range, at the outside limit, but I think he's in range and I don't think I'm going to get these birds any closer. There's too many, they're going to make me, and they seem to avoid this thick wood line, not wanting to leave the river's edge.

I roll up on my left side in the briars, ease my ole twelve ga. through the bushes out in front of me, lay back on my belly with the gun to my shoulder, take a bead on that big gobbler's head and fire.

I roll 'em right into the river and with the range so great I shoot 'em again.

Turkeys go everywhere, up river, over my head, down river, across the river, everywhere!

I'm standing now, and as all the turkeys make their break I look and there's another huge gobbler standing there looking at me, guess he hadn't woke up good yet or was taking a nap when I shot.

I fire again, to kill 'em too and miss 'em clean, my shot hitting the river behind 'em.

Up he jumps and flies, and comes as straight as an arrow to me, trying to fly right through me.

All in a split second I take this in: this huge beer-barrel of a gobbler lined up dead on me, still trying to gain enough height to get over me, (me being eight to ten feet above 'em) and I'm out of bullets. I've done shot my three number sixes and ain't got no more. I've had it.

My heart falls to my stomach, but is quickly forgotten as I realize the turkey's going to fly right through me if I don't do something.

At the last second the turkey swerves slightly to the right and I swing at 'em with my gun barrel as the wind off his wings brushes my face. This huge bird lands five feet away, I could have shot 'em ten times if I'd had the shells, and walks into the woods.

My first turkey's gone too, the one I shot to start with, flown off with the rest, the sand bar's empty, white and shiny in the sun like nobody's ever been there.

Seventy steps it was, too far by almost double. I guess the bright sun fooled me on the distance, or either that many birds just blew my cool.

I was so proud of myself when I didn't shoot that first bird before daylight cause I knew he was too far and I'd rather not shoot at one than shoot and cripple it. Now I wanted to kick myself for jumping the gun on the first one and not having any shells for the second one.

My only consolation was, I knew that at the distance I shot at the first one, that I probably startled 'em more than hurt 'em with those number sixes or at least I like to think that.

What a morning.

The story's not over:

Charlie Knows and Shows His Stuff

I came out of the woods that Friday morning all dejected and disgusted with myself. I'd had two chances at those gobblers and blown 'em both. To rub my nose in it further, I'd spied an old dim road, walked down it fifty yards, heard a commotion in the treetops and watched a gobbler, the one that had attacked me, fly off.

Arriving at the truck, where Charlie and Glenn were waiting, I related what had happened to me that morning. The only thing I left out was when I jumped the turkey outta the trees on my way out.

Charlie and Glenn were pretty nice and understanding. They only laughed for about ten minutes, then went back to trying to figure out where we could go and chase another turkey.

Glenn had spied some on the other end of the farm so we loaded up in two vehicles, Glenn showing us the way.

While we're riding, I tell Charlie about jumping that bird outta the trees on my way out.

"How long ago?" he says.

"Bout an hour," I say.

Charlie starts blowing his horn at Glenn, trying to get 'em to pull over.

"The magic hour," Charlie says pretty much to himself.

"What ya mean?" "Magic Hour," I ask.

"That bird you spooked is gonna wait about an hour, checking everything out from up in a tree, and then he's going to try and get back together with the bunch."

"Glenn," Charlie hollers through the window, "We need to go back to where we just left and hunt that turkey Leo saw."

Here we go, right back to where we'd just left, get our gear and head to the hardwoods where I'd had such a frustrating morning.

I find the little dim road and show Charlie and Glenn the big pine the bird flew out of. I point out the direction the bird flew off in and Charlie asks Glenn if the river's that way.

"No," he says.

"Good," Charlie replies, "That means he's still on our side and now we're going to kill 'em."

Down the road we go in the direction the turkey flew.

"Three hundred yards," Charlie says, "Three hundred yards is all he flew and he'll light in another tree, check things out, sail down and try to get back with his buddies."

A hundred and fifty yards or so we walk down that dim road. Charlie's never been here before, never even seen the turkey I'm talking about, but seems to know right where to go as if in his own backyard.

Charlie whispers to Glenn to go set-up fifty or so yards ahead of us. He and I ease off the road to a big ole pine, set-up and Charlie yelps three times real, real soft. He waits a few seconds and yelps good and loud ending with a sharp cluck.

We hear an almost imperceptible peep ahead in the thick brush.

"He's right here on us," Charlie whispers.

I look, trying to watch everywhere at once.

Charlie yelps real soft again.

The bird answers even softer, lower, just one small cluck.

Must be a hen, I think, a small one at that by the soft sweet sound it makes.

BAM, BAM again.

We get up now, heading for the shots, the game's over when that happens, you can breathe, talk, stretch, act like a human instead of a tree stump.

But this game's been short. Ten minutes at the most. Glenn, carrying a gobbler like you don't see much, a "major turkey" as Charlie likes to say. Eleven inch beard, inch and five eights spurs as sharp as sewing needles. A beautiful bird, twenty pounds. The bird I'd shot at, the bird I'd swung at that morning, the bird that had the bad misfortune to be in the same woods as Charlie Thomas was that morning.

We shake hands all round, marvel at the bird Glenn's shot, as we do all the birds we get to look at up close and dead, and tell Charlie how turkey wise he is.

Charlie's grinning ear to ear, as happy as if he'd shot the bird himself, knowing he's legend now in Taylor County too.

The Week In Review

All the turkey stories I just related took place the third week in March, 1999. We hunted Monday thru Friday that week and had a ball. We got on

214

turkeys everyday, got to see 'em, hear 'em and somebody got to shoot at 'em everyday except Thursday.

Thursday we were in Alabama.

That morning we were surrounded by gobbling turkeys before daylight and just couldn't get in the right place.

I could have shot one off the roost before daylight but decided to give him a sporting chance. That turkey took that chance and got clean away; only to go on posted land, start gobbling again and drive me crazy cause I couldn't call 'em outta there.

Charlie got one big gobbler going, just to let that turkey sneak up on 'em, make 'em out, and fly away.

Thursday was the turkey's day and we're not complaining cause the week had been real good to us. Five different people hunted in our group that week, Charlie, Jason, Ben, Glenn and myself and everyone of us bagged a nice bird. You can't ask for much more.

Thursday we didn't shoot.

We jokingly call our trip the "Tour de kill" after the bicycle race and some of the tennis tournaments, but don't mean it in a blood thirsty sense. If we truly just wanted to "kill" turkeys we could do it all year long cause they're really thick during deer season. We have to continually remind the boys (especially the younger ones) "do not shoot the turkeys". The birds deserve more respect than to be shot with a deer rifle, out of a tree stand, over a pile of corn.

Gobbler hunting in the spring, to my way of thinking, is probably good for the birds in general. Normally we kill the dominant bird in the group, which is usually the oldest male. He breeds all the hens, keeping the "pecking order" (and I mean peck, like hard on the back of the head), keeping the younger ones away from his flock. When you kill that dominate bird it allows younger, stronger birds to move up the pecking order. Breeding more hens successfully, keeping a large strong flock.

Again, we had a heck of a week. Every once in a while things go just right, there's no explaining it. I've learned to enjoy those times and not try too hard to look for the reason, cause there's plenty of times things go just wrong.

I've Come to this Conclusion on Gobblers

Spring Gobbler season is one of my favorite times of the year. Ain't much more I'd rather do than hunt turkey.

I just love to hear 'em gobble. Love it even more when they're gobbling or yelping at me.

I've been a true sportsman, up til now, enjoying the chase as much or more than the kill. Always calling my bird, not shooting hens, (still won't do that) but I've come to a conclusion on Gobblers.

You see, gobbler hunting can be real frustrating at times. Lots and lots of times you go without seeing or hearing a thing. Getting wet, freezing, fighting mosquitoes, sweating hot on some days, thirsty, hungry, scratched by briars, startled by snakes. It's all part of it. Once in a while things go right and you get to pull the trigger.

What I'm getting around to is roosted birds.

Twice this year I've had the good fortune to be in a position, before daylight, to slip up and shoot big gobbling turkeys off the limb where they've roosted the night before.

Both times I've passed up the chance.

It would have been easy. It was still black dark, the birds were gobbling their head off, strutting up and down on the limb they were perched on. All I had to do was walk up under 'em , in the dark, and shoot.

But I wanted to give 'em a chance.

I wanted to set-up, watch the bird fly down, yelp, have 'em gobble back as many times as possible, sneak up on me and then I'd happily shoot 'em and be proud.

Both roosted birds I could have shot did me dirty. They didn't appreciate my "sportsman like conduct" one bit. They flew down in directions I hadn't figured on and were so rude as to not come when I called. They are ungrateful birds.

I'm scratching my red bugs, pulling off ticks. My feet and my ass are wet. I'm having to sit as still as death and can't even slap at the skeeters biting my nose.

I've made up my mind.

The next time I'm lucky enough to be close in, before daylight on a gobbling, roosted bird, he's coming down. They've tricked me way more times than I've ever tricked them. I'm gonna even up the odds if I ever get another chance.

I've come to this conclusion.

The Florida Net Ban and The Tragedy Of It

The State of Florida had a statewide ballot to amend the constitution to stop all net fishing in state waters.

The people of the state overwhelmingly voted to do so.

It amazed me how easily the masses could be manipulated.

It amazed me how supposedly educated, civilized, conservative people could be led like a cow with a ring in its nose, to vote on an issue they know nothing about. An issue that in a nut shell supports genocide, in a subtle way, and supports big business, pollution and the destruction of coastal habitat.

It's a tragedy.

In many ways.

Genocide. The elimination of a culture. No bullets in the head. No mass graves. No artillery fire or jets bombing but genocide none the less. Proud, independent, hard working, historical families and communities hung-out to whither, die and disappear from the loss of their livelihood from this amendment.

An industry that was the most regulated industry in the history of the world, the net fishing industry, was in Florida.

Only allowed to fish from eight a.m. on Monday to noon on Friday. Name another industry mandated by law to work only four a half days a week.

Complete closures during the run season.

Net length restrictions.

Net mesh size restrictions that changed all during the year.

Trip limits.

Before the net ban we were restricted to using only four-inch stretch mesh during run season, to catch only the very largest of mullet recommended by the State's own biologist. The State goes from that, to only two inch stretch mesh allowed, recommended by the Marine Fisheries Commission, all political appointees, that catches only undersize, juvenile fish that are worthless on the market and illegal to possess. A catch 22 I think it's called.

The genocide part of the plan is working well. The mullet skiffs have all but disappeared. There's five marine patrol boats and planes for every mullet boat.

Big Brother is on the job.

The old water front fish houses and shrimp processors are going broke fast, selling out. Condos and marinas jumping outta the ground like weeds after a rain.

Another distinct and terrible part of the tragedy is how well the powers-that-be, the engineers of the net ban, diverted the attention of all our highly educated citizens of Florida to us, the Commercial fishing industry, as the cause of the demise of some of our marine life.

Look at the facts folks.

Forty-plus million tourists a year leave their money with a select few. They leave their garbage and sewage for us, the inhabitant of this state to deal and live with.

U.S. Fish and Wildlife states that fifty percent of the state's original wetlands have been altered or destroyed since the state was settled.

Wonder if this might have had any effect on the fish, birds or wildlife.

A thousand people a day move here permanently and have been doing so for years, sucking the water outta the ground, lowering the aquifer from a hundred or two hundred feet, down to a thousand feet in some areas. Historical lakes are dry and have been dry for years. They won't hold water anymore. South Florida's out of freshwater.

Net fishing killed the everglades dead as a stone.

Ha!

Net fishing's killing all the coral in the Pennikamp State Park.

Ha!

Net fishing's polluted the St. Johns River, the Fenholloway River, Escambia Bay, Eleven Mile Creek, made the freshwater bass load up with mercury, put a nice coat of crude-oil on the bottom the St. Marks River. We killed off the brown pelican with our nets.

We killed off most the manatees, except they never found one killed by a net. They find hundreds a year dead from being run over by high-speed recreational "sports" boats.

By the way, there's over eight hundred thousand boats registered in the State of Florida. Say that again, eight hundred thousand. 800,000.

Maybe just a little tiny bit of pollution from those. Maybe just a teeny bit of stress to the fish and wildlife from all of 'em running around, playing.

More tragedy.

They took the fish. One of Mother Nature's finest resources she gives us to harvest and eat and make a living from and they gave 'em all to the "sportsman", the recreational fisherman.

They took our lives and our food and gave 'em to a select group to play with like toys.

One more tragedy.

They were brilliant.

I can't think of any other word.

The designers of the net ban did their homework. The "lobstitutes" from the Florida Conservation Association, The Florida League of Anglers, the Florida Wildlife Federation, Florida "Sportsman" Magazine, knew how to politic and work the media. They covered all the bases, closed all the loopholes. Our industry's gone. We've lost our markets even if we could figure out a way to catch fish. Last year I caught less than twenty percent of the fish I used to catch, because of the gear they make us use, and got less than half the price I used to get. Go figure. It won't work out.

Last but not least. The final tragedy.

The net ban's written in stone. We can't change it. It's not a rule, not a law, it's an amendment to the constitution of the State of Florida. All the legislators and the governor couldn't change it if they wanted to. It can be restricted further and tightened, but not loosened.

Off the subject a little, but noteworthy. I was told by a Marine Patrol Officer that during roe season the Marine Patrol had used more high-tech equipment, night vision binoculars, helicopters, planes, and man-power hours, to stop us from catching mullet, than they had used during the height of the drug smuggling days.

Curious, huh? Can't figure it out myself.

Let's all take this as a lesson. Now we know how Hitler got the German people and soldiers to do such terrible things to other people. Now we know how leaders of one country turn one ethnic group on another like Bosnia and Kosovo, just to name a couple.

They educate people. Teach 'em what they want 'em to know. Fill 'em full of lies and propaganda. Make 'em think they're doing something good for themselves and their fellow man.

Open your eyes people.

Look along your coastline. Look all around your lakes and up and down the banks of your rivers. What do you see?

Not commercial fishermen, that's for sure.

You see condos, subdivisions, manicured, fertilized, insecticided lawns. Powerplants, bridges, docks, seawalls, marinas, jet skis, sugarcane and more sugarcane, paper mills, asphalt, concrete, cars, boats, boats, boats and thousands upon thousands upon thousand of people.

Wake up Florida. You don't want all of us gone, by us I'm talking about commercial fishermen. Believe it or not we have been, and still continue to be, some of the best stewards of our watery environment. Our livelihoods depend on a constant supply of natural resources. We're the first to notice any alteration of marine life cycles. Any decline of sea life or water quality.

The developers don't notice, the tourism industry doesn't notice, the promoters and advertisers that are begging people to come down, don't notice and the many polluters damn sure don't notice any change, won't acknowledge things wrongs even when you stick it in their face.

I know.

We've stuck it in their faces about the Fenholloway pipeline and been back patted and assured by both, the polluters and the State of Florida, when they know their both wrong.

Don't be fooled again. This tragedy of the net ban is enough. I don't know if any of it can be corrected. I think everybody's still fooled enough to not care to correct it.

Look around.

Pay attention.

Don't be fooled again.

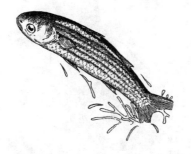

SEEIN' MYSELF   CLAY MARSHALL LOVEL   9-15-99

Seein' Myself

I got to see myself from a distance once.

It was strange driving that tunnel boat down the Goose Creek shoreline, looking at myself, my own black silhouette against the orange-pink, pre-dawn sky.

It had to be me I was seeing, standing on the short bow of that wooden skiff, cap pulled low, facing north, looking in the channel for mullet to jump. At least that's what I think I look like. I've never seen myself before.

Same slicker, same boots, same stance, even leans against the motor handle the way I do.

This clone at a distance gave me a start, shocked me for a second. Don't really know why.

Maybe it was because I didn't recognize who it was at first, the boat just like mine, the net stacked the same, fishing the same waters I fish.

Then I knew who it was.

It was Ben, my son.

It was me at a distance.

I felt proud, I felt very proud and a little sad.

Proud because Ben was on his own.

His own boat, his own gear. His own knowledge and confidence evident, just by him being there at that place, and that time.

I felt proud that someone had soaked up some of the knowledge and experience they were exposed to. Someone that worked long and hard, had enjoyed that work. Found it exciting and challenging, and had chosen to pursue it. That they were brave enough to try it on their own, knowing others would be there to observe and judge their success or failure.

I felt sad that we were a dying breed. That we wouldn't be experiencing these sunrises, waiting together on a good bunch of fish. Times were changing, we'd been pushed off the water, generations of knowledge and skill outlawed by the net ban.

All in all, I enjoyed seeing myself. It taught me a lesson. It showed me how cultures continue. How much influence we have on our children. How love of a lifestyle of adventure and challenge can be passed on.

I hope I get to see myself again someday.

The Day I Realized I Wasn't Beat

It was tough the first year.

Got tougher the next.

The net ban and the enforcement of it got hard on us in our pocket-book, and on our nerves.

The crazy laws, the helicopters hovering over us, the planes circling, under cover officers hiding in the bushes, patrol boats running us down.

To make matters worse is to have to look at all the fish swimming by. The dollars flipping and jumping, packed up, running down the shoreline in big bunches. It's like starving to death and being surrounded by fresh baked bread.

Torture.

Ya got the gear, the knowledge, the mullet, the need and ya can't get 'em.

You can only stand it so long.

You watch 'em, listen to 'em, you can almost touch 'em, they're so close and thick.

Ya gotta catch some or go crazy.

It's not natural to let that many fish go by.

The stress wears you down.

The close calls.

Constantly being on the look-out for the FMP.

Neck aches from looking up in the air for planes.

Every boat the potential enemy.

Scaring ourselves. One mullet fisherman running up on another fisherman, both of us running from each other, thinking it's the law.

Frayed nerves?

Lee Allen described it best.

"Before the net ban I couldn't thread a needle. Now, I can thread a sewing machine needle with it running wide open. That's how bad my nerves are."

The restaurant's out of fish.

Can't buy any fish.

No fish to be had anywhere.

The bay's full.

The bay's fulla fish and law.

Gotta go.

Matter of pride and necessity.

The stress starts taking its toll.

Something you loved to do, was proud to do, was excited about doing. Something you looked forward to every day of your adult life, had become a burden, a weight, a stomach-knot tying, nerve racking, headache making chore.

It almost beat me.

I almost quit it. Almost gave up.

They almost ran my ass outta the bay cause I couldn't bear the strain anymore.

But I remember the morning my soul turned around.

I remember clearly when I decided that I couldn't give it up, wouldn't give it up.

Don't know why that day, or that strike, made my mind up, but it did.

I was in Old Creek again. Rain, fog, wind, freezing, low water. No fish showing, but I knew that they were there.

The boat's shut off, I'm drifting down the channel between the bars, knowing there's a good bunch of fish lying low, beneath me.

Damn 'em all, I say to myself. To hell with 'em. I'm blind striking this hole like it's wide open, like the old days when I was free.

I pitch out the staff.

I take my time making a wide circle with the net, taking all the hole in.

I tilt my motor up, still running, to slide over the end of my net to close the circle.

I put my motor back down and start putting out more net to wind 'em down in the center. Taking my time like in the old days.

The third lap around, things start to happen. A fish hits the corkline on the outside of the circle.

A good sign in the winter. Mostly the fish hit low cause of the cold.

Two or three big mullet jump the net in the center of the circle and I'm starting to see corks shake all around.

I know they're eating it up on the lead line.

For some reason on this day, I just don't give a damn. I don't care if the helicopter comes, the plane starts dive bombing or the whole Marine Patrol roars in on me.

I'm gonna enjoy this. I'm gonna enjoy picking every fish, digging every oyster burr out, bolting every inch of this now illegal net on the boat.

Taking my time, thanking the Great Maker for every fish, every minute I've gotten to spend on His bountiful sea.

A weight lifts off me. A rare peacefulness takes over. The fish are beautiful. Old Creek's beautiful on that grey cloudy day. I'm in my element, working but relaxed. I don't know why.

I realize something.

I realize I'm not quitting. Won't quit. They can't make me quit. Bob Nichols told me one time and I'll never forget it.

"A real fisherman can take his shirt and learn how to catch fish with it if he's a mind to."

I'm living by that code now.

I'm taking what little the damn state of Florida and the sorry, stupid, politically biased marine fisheries commission has left us and we're gonna show 'em.

They can't whip us.

They can throw anything they want at us and they can't beat us.

I almost quit.

They almost won.

The millennium's right around the corner, the year 2000.

I'm still here. My boys are still hanging with me. We're still surviving, catching enough fish to get by and we'll still be doing it when all those sorry SOB's that tried to stomp us out, are all dead and gone from old age.

We're right.

They're wrong and they know it.

We'll survive.

They can't beat us.

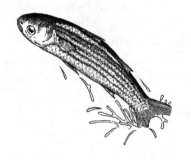

An Owl

I watched an owl tonight.

It was cold. A quick change in the weather as only North Florida knows in February. Hard Nor'easter, cloudy, bright moon peeking between the dark clouds as they flew by. Dampness penetrating the best coats. A spooky, uncomfortable, better-to-be indoors type of night.

I had closed the restaurant and was checking out the boats in our canal, mostly looking at our airboat and thinking what a mullet catching machine it was.

I turned around to look out into the creek and noticed an extension to the piling that Coot's boat was tied to. A feathery oblong extension.

It took me a second or two to realize I was looking at an owl. Still, but fluffy, its feathers on its back and head lifting in that cold damp wind, like the long gray hairs on an old man's neck, like mine was starting to be when I'd been without a haircut too long.

This creature seemed to pay me no mind.

It made me cold to watch that penetrating wind blow up under that old owl's feathers, it made me shiver.

He looked and acted more like a bush than a bird, the wind shaking the leaves around but not moving the bush. That bush never moved, he just continued staring down into the dark tannin-stained waters, watching for a fish I guess.

I tried to distract him.

Discreetly.

I chew tobacco, you know, so I spit a little squirt in the water.

He looked.

He looked right at me.

His round, black, dark, bottomless eyes looked right into mine.

For two seconds.

Then he resumed his cold, diligent watch into the cold, black water. The wind continuing to blow his neck and back feathers to attention, making me so cold I decided to go to bed.

Pre-Extinction

All the anthropologists and historians are missing a good opportunity. They've got a chance to study the culture of a small independent tribe of people before they become extinct. A pre-extinction study. I think they do it or have done it on certain minnows in some rivers, maybe the Dune Sparrow in Florida, but they don't seem much interested in studying pre-extinct people.

It's just like the American Indian. They were shoved around pressured in the name of development and "progress" til they started fighting back. For awhile all the Indians fought the changes. All they wanted to do was raise their families in their traditional proud way, live off the land from all the bounty provided by Nature, God, Allah, The Great Maker, Budda, Jesus, Jehovah, or whoever you want to credit it to. They fought hard but eventually eighty or ninety percent of 'em gave up, from all the pressure brought to bear. They were packed up and put on reservations and just kind of disappeared from the landscape, lifestyle and all.

That left the hard-headed, hard-core Indians, the one's we all know about. The Heroes, the Legends we now all admire for standing up to oppression, fighting to the death for what they knew was theirs and what was just and right.

They won a few small victories in their fight. We all admire them now.

But they're gone. They lost. They were harassed, observed, followed, starved and deprived of their right to hunt, fish and work. Soldiers everywhere. Government everywhere. Rules and regulations, too many to read or count.

I don't think they want to study pre-extinction. Especially in people.

It might be too revealing. It might be too easy. It might mess up the plan, the great scheme of things planned by the almighty dollar.

Let's talk about extinction.

I read somewhere a theory that makes sense.

Extinction is a natural process in the evolution of things. I think they said that at one time there were approximately five hundred million species of life on earth. (How they know beats me). Now they think there's approximately fifty million. The rest have become extinct.

Why? How?

One specie feeding off the other as it develops, or drastically changing its habitat in competition for space or resources.

One specie becoming so much more numerous or powerful that it denies another access to a resource it needs to survive.

Sounds natural, doesn't it.

Those historians and anthropologists better hurry.

The traditional commercial fishery in the state of Florida has been denied too much, for almost too long. The numerous and powerful are gobbling up the habitat and resources. One more generation and we're gone, extinct. Come down and see. We're not breeding or able to raise anymore baby commercial fisher people. The first sign of any specie becoming extinct.

We could still raise some. The resource is still there. Mother Nature still produces good crops, even though the numerous and powerful are eating up or altering most of her farmland along the shoreline and rivers.

But we're just not strong enough to get to those resources. There's not enough of us anymore. All of our tools, gear and equipment have been taken and there's just not enough of us left to get it back.

A few of us still scrap up enough food from the sea to survive on, but just barely. None of us are encouraging our young to pursue this independent way of life. It's more a matter of pride that we still do it and fight on.

It's not economically feasible.

Go to the new ways, children.

The white man ways, would say the Indian.

Get a government job, or with big corporation.

Get a desk.

Get insurance.

Get a pension.

You better hurry, you chroniclers of history and people. Ten years or so and you've lost your chance to study a culture, lifestyle and people that have been here as long as a man has been on earth. While you're at it, you might as well study the American Dream too. It's only a couple of hundred years old, but a big portion of it is going along with us.

Hurry up now, we're going extinct.

Bye.

What I Know Where Is

Over twenty years we've been chasing fish up and down the shore-line of the Northern Gulf of Mexico, chasing game in the woods too, but mostly chasing mullet.

The part of the Gulf we're in is a big delta region loaded with rivers flowing into the gulf. The St. Marks, Wakulla, Aucilla, Ecofina, Suwanee, Ochlockonee, Carrabelle, Appalachicola and Spring Creek are all rivers that pour fresh water into the sea making the rich bounty of fish, oysters and crabs.

For every river that flows out in this area there must be five thousand creeks that wind through the marsh-grass and up to the wood line. We've explored a bunch of 'em, looking for fish, but if we lived to be a thousand years old, we'd never be able to check 'em all out.

We've learned this though, this area has a lot of history, probably from the fact that the great resources that abound here have been sought after since man started walking on two feet if not before.

Here's a few of the things and places we've found in our exploring.

The old Confederate salt works sit out in a marsh north of Graves Creek. Marked now only by a few knarled cedar trees and chunks of rusted black iron from where the Yankees blew up the iron kettles cause they were too heavy to carry out.

A few years ago, we found some salt works sites that the Yankees missed over by Spring Creek, cause all the kettles were still intact. Six feet long, three feet wide, two feet deep they were, hand forged rims still show-ing signs of the hammer. Too rusty to move without destroying 'em.

We found some sites out in the marsh that we still ponder over what they are and who might have made 'em.

I think they're ancient.

I know the Indians and the Confederates used 'em to make salt but I think they were built thousands of years ago. I don't know how they got the rocks to build 'em with or where they got 'em. It'd be a tough job today to get 'em there. These sites have a pattern to 'em. They have a central mound of rocks and then they have "points" or "ramps" built in two or three or four different directions out from the central area, like a star.

I think they're ceremonial from a long, long time ago.

There's an Indian mound that uncovers on low tide. We've found tools, spear points, beautifully decorated potshards on this site.

There's a site way down east of the lighthouse that the Indians must have used for a long, long time to make flint tools, cause there's so much chipped flint that you can pick it up by the handfuls. At this same place we found a very old iron-headed ax, handle and all, buried in the bank of the creek. We found some sort of an iron spike there too.

Who?

When?

The area we're finding this stuff in is still remote and hard to get to.

How remote was it a hundred years ago or two hundred or a thousand?

We know of many obscure, murky salt-marsh creeks that suddenly turn crystal clear and fresh with sweet-water springs at the heads of 'em.

We know where springs boil up out in the bay, fresh water coming outta the ground, surrounded by saltwater.

We know where salt-water boils out in a spring of its own in a fresh water river.

There's the lone tombstone of a three-year-old girl, in a swamp, that I stumbled on by accident, hunting one time.

There's midden piles and burial mounds, some disturbed, others not.

We found part of an Indian's skull once, a backbone once, they stay put, we don't bother 'em. Don't want them bothering us.

There's some big caves, in a creek, underwater, that I know must have had human habitation thousands of years ago.

Old white-man campsites with old, old whiskey bottles, medicine bottles.

Ancient graveyards, pre-mound builders, old, old people's. I know where they are.

We know where the gators lay their eggs.

Where the manatees give birth.

Where the manatees make love.

Where the shrimp turn from larvae to baby shrimp, where they raise and grow up to eating size. Where they move to when they get big.

We know where the blue crabs molt, where they're bred, when they mature.

We know where the mullet go when the weather turns cold.

We know where the trout and redfish go on big weather changes and why.

We know where the eagles nest, how many young they have and watch 'em train 'em to fish.

The egrets, pelicans and seagulls all have their special places they lay their eggs and raise their young.

How many sea turtle nests would you like to see?

Did you know that baby porpoises cling to their mother's breast and are carried along effortlessly with the rest of the herd?

There's holes in the bay, little washes and guts that big speckled trout always gather in, year after year, laying like firewood on the bottom.

We've got a dug-out canoe spotted, just the tip end of it sticking outta the mud in the marsh grass. Nobody'll ever find it.

Wood Duck ponds, turkey roosts, buck rubs, bream and bass beds, we know where they are.

Old rock quarries, abandon grist wheels, hidden springs, lotsa things that we enjoy being around, by ourselves, not wanting to share with anyone cause it'd break the spell.

Maybe it's being selfish, but I've seen too many times, too many people knowing about something and somebody ruining it.

We tell select people about certain places, people that respect oldness and history and nature. They in turn share places and things they've discovered.

What I know where is won't amount to much at the bank, but it's sure precious to me.

About the Artwork

Clay Marshall Lovel is proud to have illustrated SPRING CREEK CHRONICLES. He currently lives in Spring Creek and is studying in the Fine Arts Program at Florida State University.

If you are interested in prints of any of the artwork contained in SPRING CREEK CHRONICLES, or you would like drawn or painted any image important to you, such as a home, cabin, animal or person, he can be contacted at **850-926-5735** or thru SPRING CREEK RESTAURANT.

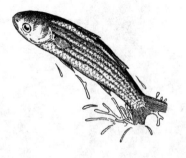

Spring Creek is an old fishing community that is virtually unchanged over the last 50 years.

It is made up of three fish houses, about 50 residents and Spring Creek Restaurant. Spring Creek Restaurant is a family owned and operated restaurant that has been serving the finest of local sea foods, much caught by our own boats, since 1977.

Soft shell crab caught in our local waters fresh shrimp, bulldozer lobster and crab cakes made from our local blue crabs, stone crabs in season, mullet roe, and grilled jumbo shrimp are a few of our items, along with our homemade chocolate peanut butter pie and the best hush puppies you ever had. Come enjoy dinner with us and look at Florida as it used to be.

Be sure to bring your own beer, liquor or wine because we don't serve any, but you can bring it into the restaurant.

Directions - from Tallahassee - follow State Road 363 to U.S. 98 - turn right on 98, go 6 miles to State Road 365, turn left and follow until it dead ends. That will be Spring Creek.

Hours of Operation:
Sunday - 12-9 p.m. • Monday - Closed
Tuesday - Closed • Wednesday - 5-9:30 p.m.
Thursday - 5-9:30 p.m. • Friday - 5-10:00 p.m.
Saturday - 12-10 p.m.

TALLAHASSE
*
363
US 98
365
*SPRING CREEK

Attention Fisherman

Have your own place in Spring Creek

Furnished room with A / C, TV, beds, full- bath, place to store your boat, water access, boat ramp, dock space, ice, cleaning facilities, cook room all included. Flats type boat preferred. Red fish, trout, tarpon, fresh water fishing, duck hunting all available in one place, 3 month minimum lease.

Ask at the restaurant or contact:

Spring Creek Restaurant
33 Ben Willis Road
Crawfordville, Florida 32327
(850) 926-3751

"Spring Creek Chronicles" may be obtained by contacting the Restaurant

For Information on Real Estate anywhere in the North Florida Area, Contact

BENJAMIN B. LOVEL

850-570-1293

EXPERIENCED IN RESIDENTIAL, RECREATIONAL AND COMMERCIAL TRANSACTIONS